REFLECTIONS FROM
THE *Powder Room* ON
THE
Love Dare

Writers: Shae Cooke, Tammy Fitzgerald, Donna Scuderi, Angela Rickabaugh Shears

Cover designer, and page layout: Dominique Abney

DESTINY IMAGE® PUBLISHERS, INC.

P.O. Box 310, Shippensburg, PA 17257-0310

"Speaking to the Purposes of God for This Generation and for the Generations to Come."

This book and all other Destiny Image, Revival Press, MercyPlace, Fresh Bread, Destiny Image Fiction, and Treasure House books are available at Christian bookstores and distributors worldwide.

For a U.S. bookstore nearest you, call 1-800-722-6774.

For more information on foreign distributors, call 717-532-3040.

Or reach us on the Internet: www.destinyimage.com

ISBN 10: 0-7684-3059-3

ISBN 13: 978-0-7684-3059-2

For Worldwide Distribution, Printed in the U.S.A.

1 2 3 4 5 6 7 8 9 10 11 / 13 12 11 10 09

TABLE OF CONTENTS

PREFACE

When venturing into any powder room there is always a feeling of relief...and apprehension. Will it be clean is top of mind for me. Then, how about the amenities. Are the essentials there? Will there be clear, clean water to refresh myself? Will there be enough light to reveal my flaws so I can cover them with powder? And how about the "extras"? Will there be a smiling lady there to hand me a nice soft towel to dry my face and hands? Will the seats in front of the mirror be comfortable enough to make me want to sit a little longer?

I thought the same things as I wandered into The Powder Room online chat space...

INTRODUCTION

"What is the use of a book," thought Alice [in Wonderland],
"without pictures or conversations."

What's more fun than reading a book? Discussing it with friends...or even strangers who become friends!

Four of us happened upon The Powder Room, an online reading place where women discuss, dissect, and dish out some diverse thoughts about best-selling books.

A book is not only a friend—it makes friends when people are drawn into a conversation about it. Although as different from each other as colors of lipstick, hair, and fingernail polish, we felt a divine connect through humor, personality quirks, and a common desire to gain momentum toward our God-given destiny.

Here we review books written by those who have traveled similar roads and triumphed, or who have taken different directions and found transformation in areas of spirituality, setbacks, and relationships. We try on the principles and teachings in the books for size and fit, and then share what works or what doesn't.

As an eclectic group of animated and transparent women, ours becomes a journey of tears and fears, laughter and joy, as we find the courage to rise above the bling to find God's pearls of wisdom and truth. As we search for answers and insight in the mall...err...halls of our dreams, many times the book being reviewed becomes our catalyst.

We had fun with our online discussions and decided to share our banter, "deep" thoughts, and yadayadayada. For those of you who don't have time to read an entire good book—read it through us! Of course we rambled a bit throughout, but that's the great thing about friends, right? Calgon, take us away!

Reflections from the Powder Room on The Love Dare is the first book in The Powder Room Series. *The Love Dare* was featured in the movie, *Fireproof,* and is a 40-day challenge that strengthens the marriage relationship. Each day defines what love is and provides practical and biblically based principles to apply.

PART I

Love and Life

THE DARE

Angela

The Love Dare. Hmmm...I haven't been dared since elementary school when Eddie dared me to ride my big sister's bike with handlebar brakes down the steep alley near our homes. A bloody bare foot and many years later I'm still squeamish about dares—but here goes!

Although I have a 31-year-long "successful" marriage, there is always room for improvement, right? And like when you first start a diet, it's fun to drag a friend along for the ride. Since my husband pretended not to hear me when I asked him about taking "the dare" with me, I decided to visit The Powder Room and chat here about the book and the 40-day journey that hopefully will lead me to the Promised Land of continued marital bliss...with a man with selective hearing.

Day 1 is focused on love being patient. Well, I must admit

that I've been trying my husband's patience for years! But he's a good sport and when I see his eyes glazing over I realize that anything more that I add to the conversation will not be heard and/or appreciated.

"Few of us do patience very well and none of us do it naturally." This nugget from the book fell hard on my hard head. I agree completely. Whether sitting in traffic, standing in line at Starbucks, or waiting for a "real person" to answer the computer help line, my fuse is not as long as it should be.

In compliance with "Today's Dare" I will honor one of my dad's frequent admonitions, "Angela, if you can't say something nice, don't say anything."

Donna
◇◇◇◇◇◇◇◇◇◇

And then there's the "speak the truth in love" command. Alas, a topic for another day. This patience as "permission to be human" thing is huge. It's not even lunchtime and I've already inadvertently revoked permission from two unsuspecting humans who crossed my path. For a single, unattached baby-boomer who didn't wake up to find her husband's socks on the floor, that's quite an accomplishment!

So, message received! I'm *s-t-r-e-t-c-h-i-n-g* to wrap my all-too-short arms around this very big idea—and I'm repentant about my mutterings to the absent-minded soul who ran the stop sign and failed (just barely) to broadside my law-abiding, freshly-washed automobile. And for the landlord whose ice-removal practices are wanting, today is "Permission to Be Human Day"—even though twelve perfectly good eggs are splattered beside the spot where I began my skate across the parking lot.

Ha! Hopefully someone caught that performance on video, even if I didn't think it was funny at the time. But, seriously, as a card-carrying human being, patience tries my patience. That's what happens when perfection (which is so obviously unattainable) moves too high up my priority list.

I'm with you, Angela! I'm taking on today's dare. For me it says, "Donna, give everyone you meet a chance to be imperfectly human."

Tammy

"We are born with a lifelong thirst for love."

That, I can say with assurance, is absolutely true. I think the thing that makes it most obvious to me is how happy I am to let my cat fall asleep on my lap (taking the circulation in my legs with him), all in hopes that someday that little kitty heart will adore me for it.

As I begin reading through a book that is primarily written for married people, I can't help feeling that my usual reaction to most of what I read will probably be something along the lines of, "Oh, really? Is that how it is?" After all, how should I know? I think I must be *the* most confirmed single person I've ever met. When it comes to working on my marriage...

well, I'm not. I don't have one.

What I *do* have is my own little slice of humanity—a sampling of this imperfect race that I happen to come in contact with and relate to as one of its own. And Donna, I'm with you on this being "Permission to be Human Day." In fact, I think I'll need to extend the Permission to be Human celebration for more than a day—maybe a month would be more like it. :-) By that time, I'll be living this first-day dare of patience daily...won't I?

Honestly, I've never thought of myself as an impatient person, and most people I know probably wouldn't pin me as one either. But I think the truth of the matter—after just a little bit of close attention to the mish-mash of stuff going on in my head—is probably that I *am* an impatient person, I'm just not a very confrontational one. But just because I don't *show* my irritation doesn't mean it's not there, damaging my spirit and my ability to relate openly and lovingly with those in my life.

So, three deep breaths and count to ten, Tammy...and most importantly, pray and keep a close watch over my own spirit.

For a single gal, this book for married folks is already proving to be a challenge.

Shae

I need permission to be human for more than a day! Being in a long-distance relationship with the love of my life requires a lot of patience. "Doug" definitely has more of it than I do.

I admire patient people. Michelangelo was one. It took him four years of backbreaking work atop a scaffold 65' in the air to paint his fresco masterpiece on the ceiling of the Sistine Chapel in Rome. "Genius," he said, is "eternal patience." Well, strip off my brown highlights and pour on the blonde. That would place my IQ a little higher than a lima bean at times. I prefer to think of patience as a trait of the wise.

Random Acts of Kindness

Angela

The last time I saw the word *kindness* was on the bumper of an old, rusty Volkswagen bus—Practice Random Acts of Kindness. Well, maybe more of us should have that bumper sticker.

I liked reading that "kindness thinks ahead"—which is a key ingredient in most happy relationships. For instance, I think ahead about replacing the toilet paper before the last sheet is hanging off the roll. My husband, on the other hand, is still not sure if this key applies to him. He thinks ahead to turn down the bed in the evening while I'm still pounding the keyboard—but I'm never quite sure if he's turning it down for me or our 80-pound Old English Sheepdog who chooses to sleep smack dab between us most nights!

We really do try to perform random acts for each other. He takes the garbage out, and I actually make dinner once, maybe twice, a week. I offer to drive to the restaurant and he offers to pay. I clean the house and he cleans the bathrooms. And the real secret to a good marriage...we do our own laundry!

I was seriously convicted reading Proverbs 31:26, "She opens her mouth in wisdom, and the teaching of kindness is on her tongue." Wow—I doubt I'll ever feel as if wisdom drips from my mouth or that I'm qualified to teach kindness.

Yea, I think I'll try and find one of those bumper stickers for my car.

Tammy

I started the chapter on kindness thinking, "Oh, awesome. It's already getting easier." Because I'm kind. Of *course* I'm kind. Tra-la-la, I'm amazing at *that* one.

And then I read, "Kindness creates a blessing." Imagine a bit of a pause here.

Never mind, I'm not kind. I'm nice. I'm pleasant enough for people to seem to like being around me, but that doesn't mean I consistently, consciously create blessings for them. I don't have one other person with whom I share my life intimately, so I think it can be easy for me to get away with showing up and being nice when I want to be, then scampering off when I'm tired of the company. (That's an introvert for you!)

But even when I'm at my best with people, I don't think I can honestly say that I think ahead and proactively do things to create blessings for them. I'm decent company—I'm *nice*—and then I bow out and hope that someone else does the real blessing. That's a rather unpleasant realization for me.

I need to be more careful. As a single person without a spouse to focus on, I feel like I should be able to spread a little kindness around to so many people. Perhaps what I need is a little accountability—someone to ask me who I've blessed lately. Or a roommate. A good roommate who didn't let me get away with anything might be just the thing.

Donna

Uh-oh. I have some 'splaining to do.

I do kindness, but does that make me kind? My parents raised my brother and me to be respectful and considerate, honest and accountable...all that good stuff. Some of it has to count toward my kindness quotient, right?

But, as the clanging cymbal rings loudly in my heart, the answer is a resounding "Yes—and no." I'm not into self-bashing (or anybody-bashing), and in all fairness I am a devoted friend. I have an active compassion for the hurting. I honor others.

Yet, I have to consider Tammy's question: Am I *kind* or just *nice*? Do I (ever?) boil down kindness to such a degree that its active ingredients evaporate into thin air? Are gentleness, helpfulness, willingness, and initiative evident in my life or do I sometimes settle for being a big, yellow smiley face, a dose of Love Lite?

Take helpfulness, for example. There are certain tasks for which I am not wired. Like throwing parties, bridal showers, that sort of thing. Being responsible for such events is anathema to me. I'd sooner enter the witness protection program—*anything* would be better than organizing a bridal shower. I would plead to contribute in any number of other ways. I could list them for you in a New York minute. Yes, but...that's not the point because being helpful means "meeting the needs of the moment."

So, is *Bridal Showers for Dummies* out yet?

Shae

Angela, you really do have a gem of a husband. There isn't a hint of a toilet seat dilemma anywhere in your relationship! Alas, it is hard to be kindhearted to a man who leaves the seat up in the middle of the night.

So how do we lovingly approach a matter that bothers us to someone we love. A wise Bible proverb says, "A kindhearted woman gains respect." We show our loved ones kindness no matter how much they annoy us at times. According to *The Love Dare's* ingredient list for kindness, look for ways to compromise and accommodate. I guess that means my random acts of kindness will be to leave the toilet seat up after I am finished. No, I have resolved to make that a deliberate act of kindness, and then maybe, just maybe, I'll gain a little R.E.S.P.E.C.T around here! *wink, grin!*

And Donna girl, there is something worse than organizing a bridal shower—and that's having to walk down the aisle as a bridesmaid in a puffy hot pink taffeta number that you hate and have to pay for!

3

TALKIN' TURKEY

Donna

Who me? Selfish?

Guilty as charged. I'm sure friends or loved ones could oblige with examples of how I inadvertently trampled their emotions at some point or other. Not that I'm a particularly insensitive person (although, I do amaze myself at times). And yes, encouraging others and embracing their uniqueness *are* core principles of mine.

That said, let's talk turkey: I'm a turkey, too, and more often than I probably realize. I'm not 100% sure you could build a hit reality show around the tidbits tucked away in my Selfishness Hall of Fame; neither am I certain that you couldn't.

So here's the rub: selfishness *is.* It runs on autopilot. And need I remind myself that it's virtually invisible from the center of one's own universe. The question becomes, how much me-centered-ness has issued forth from the Throne of Myself today? And if "nobody knows you as well as your spouse," am I honestly seeking sources of real-time feedback, the kind married folks enjoy?

Did I say *enjoy*? Anyway, speaking of singles, Tammy, your words about being "*the* most confirmedly single person" you've ever met caused me to shout, "Move over, girl, you've got company!"

Hmmm...that could be yet another example of me at the center of my world.

Angela

Let me just start out by saying that yes, Donna and Shae, there IS something worse (in a good way, if that's possible) than planning a bridal shower or wearing a horrid pink taffeta dress...planning a wedding for 200-plus guests, 150 of whom you have never met, who descended from various la-de-dah New York City suburbs to your home on a quiet, oak-tree lined road in the country for a formal full-course, catered, sit-down dinner on your front lawn with a band from "the City" set up under your weeping cherry tree! And did I mention that the bride's gown cost more than our first AND second cars AND that she was living in and working as a teacher in the Bronx at the time leaving all the million details to dear old Mom?!

Hmmm, does that count for a gigantic act of selflessness on my part?

When I think of selflessness, Mother Teresa comes immediately to mind, then next my mother and father. For examples, every few weeks my dad—who never missed a day of work and also had a side business—would drive the only African American man who lived in our small town 11 miles to a barber who would cut his hair. My mother volunteered to crank out the weekly church bulletins on an old mimeograph machine tucked away in the corner of our dining room, and she was actively involved in community fundraising—the real kind that helped real people.

These acts of selflessness were second nature to them.

Now that we are empty-nesters, I must admit that my life is rarely inconvenienced. Sure I give money to our church and send money to local, national, and international charities, but I'm not "out there" actually getting my hands dirty in the streets of India or even at the mimeograph machine.

Lord, may acts of selflessness become second nature to me too.

Tammy

Oh, I'm selfish. There is absolutely no question about that.

This must mean that I don't really *love* my poor cat the way I always tell him I do. For here I sit, and all he wants is for me to get up and open the door for him—he has some feline business to attend to, probably—yet I don't move. I'm comfy in my warm chair at the moment, so my cat is crying his little heart out while I love myself more than him.

Perhaps I'm being dramatic. Certainly my relationship with my cat isn't nearly as significant as my relationship with another human being or with God. Still, my cat has never hurt me or disappointed me the way most people have or will. So if there were one creature that had never harmed me or done anything to challenge my ability to love them, I think it would have to be this cat. And look how far that gets him. He's still meowing at me to put him out.

Donna is right—selfishness is automatic. It's my default setting, and no matter how many times I try to change it, it automatically resets. Lord, reprogram me.

Now, if you'll excuse me, I have to go let my cat out.

Shae

Meow! Tammy, by now you've let the cat out and he has completely forgiven you! Does the cat have a name?

Don't be so hard on yourself—you're growing as we all are. May I remind you of the little boy who watched fascinated as his mother smoothed cream on her face?

"Why do you do that, mommy?"

"To make myself beautiful," said his mother, who then began removing the cream with a tissue.

"What's the matter," asked the little boy. "Giving up?"

Ha! Not on your life! That's why I'm still here in the powder room and just about to slather on some selflessness. I already feel more beautiful.

I heard it through the grapevine that Chelsea Noble, actor Kirk Cameron's real-life bride, was allowed on the set for the final kissing scene in *Fireproof* so that Kirk could stay true to his wedding vows and kiss no one other than his wife. He wrote on her heart that day an incredibly selfless message— "I'm thinking of you, I care about you, you mean the world to me."

SAY WHAT?!

Donna

Ahhh...a sweet memory just poked through the depths of consciousness to the front of my mind. Hope you gals don't mind if I bask in its warmth for just a sec.

Talk about thoughtful! My first true love, I'll call him *Jon,* was thoughtfulness personified. He was as imperfect as the next guy, but never missed an opportunity to demonstrate his love through creative, affirming actions.

In our college years, Jon and I attended different schools with campuses several miles apart. After the day's classes, I'd trudge back to my white Corvair, which, typically, was parked six or eight blocks from campus. Nine times out of ten, I'd find a note or drawing from Jon waiting for me on the windshield. Heartened, I would release from the grip of the wiper blade the weathered page Jon had so carefully pinned there hours earlier.

Always I would stand amazed, absorbing these tokens of Jon's love into the very marrow of my being. His thoughtfulness had cost him something. Just finding my car on the streets of New York City was an undertaking!

But Jon took inconvenience in stride. Much like our heavenly Father, Jon didn't struggle with the logistics of thoughtfulness. It was part of who he was.

For me, today's dare is to be more like them.

Tammy

Oh Donna, you had an awfully nice boyfriend there! Thoughtful, indeed! Must have been a pleasant experience. ^_^

The most interesting part of this chapter to me was the discussion about how men and women communicate in relationships. Of course, it wasn't my first time hearing about the feminine tendency to "hint" and the challenges this typically presents for the poor man who struggles if things aren't spelled out for him. This communication issue is very believable for me, even with my lack of experience, because I see it absolutely everywhere. I liked the twist this book added though: the idea that a woman being a "hinter" can be a good thing, because it gives the man even more opportunities to demonstrate thoughtfulness when he has to work hard to figure out what she wants.

I was curious about something though; maybe those with more experience can throw some light on this for me. See,

I've always considered myself extremely plain-speaking. In fact, I had to work hard to curb that natural tendency of mine toward bluntness. So I kind of wonder, if I ever did get married, would I end up being too clear and robbing my guy of chances to be thoughtful? Or (here's the real question), would I discover that I'm way more cryptic to him than I thought myself to be?

Any experience from the married front?

Angela

Well, Tammy, since you asked...there is no such thing as being "too clear" for a man. The clearer the better. Case in point: Because I didn't come right out and tell my husband that I expected mushy, sentimental cards for my birthday and anniversary, it took him 2-3 years to catch on. For days after a special day, I would sulk around the house in silent mode. But after he actually "got it," it become too much of a "thoughtful routine" because one anniversary I opened the envelope to find a romantic-looking couple who were of a completely different race. Ummm, obviously he only saw Happy Anniversary and didn't notice anything else about the card. Men.

"A husband should...learn to be considerate of her unspoken messages." If I took that advice seriously, we probably wouldn't have had our second daughter, a house, a car, me a career, or any Christmas gifts other than what the guys on talk radio sell (although I really do like this year's pajama-gram flannels!).

In truth, after this many years of marriage, we have pretty much perfected our periodic acts of thoughtfulness to accommodate each other's quirks. God has blessed us richly. And, yes, I actually speak that quite clearly and quite often... just in case he's not listening for those "unspoken messages."

Shae

How about thoughts from the "married before" front Tammy? Being straightforward has its merits but there is still a chance of miscommunication, whether we are vague and opaque or clear and precise. Somewhere there has to be a place of connection to communicate our desires.

One night my husband asked me if I wanted to go out for dinner. I told him, "Yes, awesome." He asked me what I wanted. I told him it didn't really matter, just going out was nice. He lamented, "Why can't you just make up your mind." So I did, suggesting all sorts of restaurants but he pooh-poohed them all. Finally, I hit the jackpot with an Italian restaurant. I had to go through all of that when he could have just said, "Get dressed honey, we're going to La Pergola!"

"ME ME"

Angela

◇◇◇◇◇◇◇◇◇◇◇

When I think of rude, I think "Roseanne." Although our house-with-children years were chaotic, we weren't deliberately rude to each other. Physically and emotionally exhausted and wildly exasperated at times, yes...but not rude.

During the "terrible twos" (the stage that actually lasts until age 22), we taught our children to "share, be nice, take your turn, don't yell, don't wipe your nose on your sleeve, say please and thank you," and all those things that you hope and pray will stay with them throughout life. So far, so good.

As husband and wife, we too try to keep these terrible-two's truths top o'mind. So far, so good.

Shae

My marriage went through the "me me" struggle stage.

Stage one was wedded bliss where we transcended the "I" and understood the concept of "We."

Enter the stage of the Great Rude Awakening, the "let's test the waters" in this sea of love stage. It knocked the princess who'd thought she married the prince of her dreams right off of her happily-ever-after throne, and I'm sure he wondered more than once why he fit me with that glass slipper. The slipper shattered. Our marriage did not survive the testy time, and I felt like the ugly step sister.

I am convinced though that those terrible-two years do not have to be so rough. In my new relationship, we are looking to God constantly to make us His new creations, so that when we are finally together, we can circumnavigate those testy waters and be the kind of couple who can make the adjustments and commitments necessary for a joyful, happy home life. We also pray together every day. It is amazing what a minute or two talking to the Lord together does to build that important spiritual bond—it is not easy to stay angry with a prayer partner, even if he is a toad sometimes!

Donna

Shae, I'm moved by your story and reminded that both sin-

gles and couples endure disappointment. Oh, and Angela—
"Roseanne" was not my cup of tea, either.

So, why didn't I hit "surf" on my trusty clicker when a favorite rerun of mine was preempted by a rude, crude reality show? I confess: the teaser hooked me. A family that prided itself on being rude was getting a substitute mom who happened to be an etiquette specialist. Who could resist the irony? The Etiquette Evangel spends two weeks with The Uncouth Clan.

There were issues aplenty on both sides, but since "rude" is today's buzzword, The Uncouth Clan takes center stage. They oozed disrespect and wallowed unaware in its toxic stream. The Etiquette Evangel was determined to expose the poison and present an alternative approach.

The clash was titanic; but in time, The Uncouth Clan dipped a cautious toe in the sweet river of mutual respect. Bam!— they were hooked! They discovered the joy of living in an "atmosphere of honor."

Glad I stuck around for the ending.

GUILTY AS CHARGED

Tammy

I wonder if women are unfairly stereotyped as the ones who don't communicate clearly. Seems to me that men can be just as guilty of not saying what they mean.

Or maybe they need to read up on the Day 6 lesson—"Love is not irritable." At least, it looks that way a bit. ^_^ Of course, we can probably all take this lesson to heart, especially regarding the dangers of stress and the importance of that Sabbath day of rest. (Coming up with that was just plain smart, Lord!) It's almost hard to really make yourself rest one day a week when you're really busy. I know my usual reaction to a "free" day is, "Oh look, a little bit of time to do the million and one things I didn't have time for this week!" Oh dear.

And my cat's name, by the way, is Kitty—nothing special. But he almost never gets irritated with me...he must really love me! Right? LOL.

Shae

Oh to have a cat's leisurely uncomplicated life! Well, not really. Being a cat does have its disadvantages, like being prey to coyotes, especially up here on my mountain in the Pacific Northwest—but I won't go there and ruin Kitty's (or your) day.

I think we risk the enemy's hungry jaws when we are overly anything. What I unpacked from this bulging chapter was the realization that I am a sprinter, and often end my days not finishing anything well. Racing from here to there, starting one project without finishing the next, being a "yes" person when I cannot take on one more thing—it all compounds as stress and thoughtlessness and then I'm enemy bait. Being overly busy puts so much pressure on me that sometimes I snap when I do not mean to, and then of course I spend all night on my knees asking God to forgive me for not being a better mother, sister, or friend, for wreaking havoc on another's joy, on that "atmosphere of honor," that Donna so beautifully termed. Condemnation sets in—and that is the enemy's primo tactic for taking me down.

Donna

Kendrick advocates being "a joy instead of a jerk." Great advice! Irritable people irritate people. They tend to sow the wind and reap whirlwinds, often of their own making.

Years ago, I had a co-worker, a woman possessed of many fine qualities, but prone to biting off the heads of her workmates. Being around her was to be "near the point of a knife" as Kendrick put it. She demanded kid-glove treatment and got it from those who, not so surprisingly, were more comfortable placating her than loving her.

Eventually bitterness and ill-will surrounded her. Then, some months after my departure, I learned that the prickly prima donna had been bumped to the unemployment line. Maybe if she hadn't burned so many bridges...

Lord, help me to "be a joy and not a jerk." And when I encounter the "point of the knife," help me to be part of the solution.

Angela

Picture this. My husband and daughters sitting around the kitchen table where a birthday cake and presents were arranged. Their eyes were sparkling with "We've got a birthday secret." As I opened the handmade-in-art-class gifts and cards and the inevitable fuzzy slippers, I noticed two small boxes that escaped my trained gift-detecting senses. Hmmm. As I reached for the boxes, "the fam" started to laugh and giggle. Hmmm. Must be something wonderful—something I'm going to love!

The first bow was pulled off, the paper ripped away, and the small plastic bottle extracted from the box. By now my family was roaring with laughter as I read the label on the bottle: "Take 2 capsules daily to stop PMS irritability." What? I flashed a faux smile and opened the other gift. "Grouch Pills—take as often as necessary—please!" Huh?

Tears ran down my face. How could I have missed the impression I was making at home? I recently asked my daughter if she remembered this incident. "Ah, gee, yea, mom. After you started crying, I made a 'note to self'—don't buy Mom practical joke gifts—she won't get it."

Fortunately, this story has a happy ending...surgery and HRT!

CHIGGERS ANYONE?

Shae

Gag gifts annoy me, Angela. Usually people give them to me because they say I am hard to buy for. That's just not so!

These "milestone" presents are quite popular. I remember the "over the hill" stuff I received on my "Lordy Lordy look who's forty" birthday. Ha ha to the person who thought the package of Depends rip roaringly funny or to the person who called me a "living fossil." What's to come this July 25th when I turn um, nifty 30?

Focusing on someone's weakness can really magnify their faults. I recall a time a few years ago when I visited a friend's homestead in rural Kentucky. He warned me about chiggers; pesky little bugs that purportedly burrow under the skin and surface a few days later leaving crater-type holes as they chew their way out. Ewwwe! But he only warned me *after* I had been sitting in the grass in my shorts by the pond fishing all day! We don't have chiggers in the West, so you can understand how much it freaked me out when I got home and it seemed those nasty critters started to munch their way through my skin, in places even "where the sun don't shine!"

It took me weeks to get over the trauma; my magnifying glass and tweezers were always close by because every bump I thought for sure was a chigger about to eat me alive. Powder Puffs, you do know where I am going with this, don't you? *grin*

Tammy

Shae, that is poignantly illustrative and...horrifying. Especially to someone like me with a severe bug phobia.

Anyway! I think one of the coolest things about appreciation is that you discover more wonderful things about a person if you live in a place of appreciating them. I'm sure it works the other way around too. The more time you spend either thinking highly or thinking poorly of a person, the more you discover about them that fits in with the way you are thinking about them.

I think there have been times when I couldn't stop thinking depreciatively of a friend or acquaintance. It is terribly destructive; in that kind of a place, you see even the good things about a person in a negative light.

At the same time, I know I have friends whom I love to appreciate. And I certainly agree with this chapter—the knowledge of their failings is still there, but all those bad things I know about that person don't matter, because I love them. And you know, it's not like I want to pretend those weaknesses don't exist. I want them to be covered in love. It makes the love and the relationship so much stronger than it would be if I naively pretended they didn't exist.

Angela

Oh to spend more time appreciating people.

We went to a Christmas party this year where people know my husband as a retired Army officer, retired federal government staff, and now a custom framer and local codes enforcement officer. They also know him as a fun-loving guy who makes them laugh, a professional, and an honest man through and through. Like you mentioned, Tammy, when you allow them to, some of the good things about a person can show up in a negative light. When thinking about my husband from a *lack of appreciation,* his sense of humor leans toward a hee-hawing good time and his honesty and integrity keep him from actually making any profit from his framing business. When I focus on *appreciating* his quirkiness, I enjoy and admire these traits.

And Shae...thanks for the bug story. Kentucky is now off the list of places to see before I die.

Donna
◇◇◇◇◇◇◇◇◇◇◇

Houston, we have a problem—chiggers have taken up residence under somebody else's skin. I won't mention any names, but her initials are Donna S.

As OCD as I can be about being fair and reasonable and blah blah blah blah blah...I have provided luxury accommodations for a bug! I built my "case" on the following thesis: *I feel that you, my valued friend, are not being frank about something important and it has shaken my trust.*

Note to self: it doesn't matter what your friend does or doesn't do. The bigger issue is this: as long the chigger is under *your* skin, you're the problem.

Unacceptable. Like the adorable rabbits that chewed a gaping hole in my car's electrical system. I didn't realize they were at work in my engine—probably had been for months—until my dashboard lit up like a Christmas tree and I lost engine power while driving uphill in the snow. The solution? Five hundred bucks and a good spray of rabbit repellent.

Uhhh...I hope I don't have to spray fox urine on my chigger hill.

GREEN-EYED MONSTERS

Shae

I am glad for today's challenge to destroy the (thankfully) little bitty list I created yesterday of my mate's negative attributes. Writing it left a bitter taste in my mouth, and honestly, I got to thinking more about those chigger hills than I should have. In contrast, listing his positive attributes was like downing a glass of honey; it was so sweet to my lips.

Tammy

"You don't usually get jealous of disconnected strangers." What an interesting point about jealousy! I don't think I had quite realized that, but it's so true. My goodness, there are celebrities out there—we almost can't avoid hearing about them—who have riches and talents that leave us "ordinary" people behind in the dust. But in the end, I don't know them personally, so it doesn't bother me.

I can only imagine how hard it must be, then, to keep jealousy out of a marriage. I mean, no other person could be closer. And their successes could be the most needling...if you allow room in your heart and relationship for jealousy.

On the other hand, what a cool relationship it can be if two people cement themselves together to the point where they really celebrate the successes of each other as their own! Talk about unity! Not to mention, you get to celebrate double the successes throughout life.

It sure makes jealousy look a little illogical and silly, if you think about it.

Angela

Thankfully jealously has never been an issue for us. We have always been each other's biggest fan club members. I remember his reaction when I asked him what he thought of the idea of opening a craft store. "GO FOR IT!" We did and had an enjoyable three years of teaching painting classes, basketweaving, scherenschnitte, flower arranging, etc. I remember his reaction when I asked him what he thought of me finishing my college degree. "GO FOR IT!" As I attended classes at the University of Hawaii Manoa with thousands of beautiful young Japanese, Korean, Chinese, Taiwanese, Filipino, Samoan, Malaysian, Vietnamese, mainland, and local students, he cheered me on even though I felt out-of-place and out-of-age. At graduation, his smile was the biggest.

And when I tried on different careers, his continual vote of confidence helped make me a successful Director of Communication for a nonprofit organization, newspaper reporter, and owner of a writing and editing business.

He has always been in my corner—and I his. As co-workaholics, we are not jealous of each other's accomplishments, we spur each other on.

Donna

Oh no! I'm jealous! Or am I just rabidly inspired by the quality of your marriage, Angela? (I'll go with the latter. :-) It's the kind of relationship we singles dream of having, that is, if we're still dreaming.

Who hasn't tasted the artificially-sweetened green glob called *envy*? Speaking for myself, I've been on both sides of the sticky mess. I've read about Cain a zillion times and wondered haughtily, "Dude, what were you thinking?" Then, without missing a beat, I've jumped into his bloodstained sandals. Like when a divorced friend remarried and I spewed my not-so-veiled complaint: "Okay God...think You might select for me just *one* spouse before Jesus returns?"

Like every other human, I've been on the receiving end of jealousy, too. Ever had a friend or co-worker flash a saccharin smile when you shared a piece of *really good* news, say a promotion or some other big break? Ouch!

In the end, I'd rather be on the receiving end than the dishing end of jealousy. One delivers a momentary sting, an opportunity for personal growth, and a generous helping of God's grace. The other just gives the chiggers some fresh flesh to work with.

9

YOUR BEST (PRADA) FOOT FORWARD

Angela

"You can tell a lot about the state of a couple's relationship from the way they greet one another." That statement just about wraps up the reason why "they" say a dog is a person's best friend. Maggie greets us (Mr. Man and The Mrs.—we refuse to allow her to call us Dad and Mom) with the same enthusiasm and ecstatic short-tail wags no matter what her day was like, no matter how tired she is. She is happy to see us no matter if the squirrels outside tormented her all day, no matter if her hair is a mess, or her food bowl was temporarily empty.

"Hi! I'm SO glad you're home! WOW! I love you! HELLO! I'm SO happy you came to see me! GREETINGS! What a sight for sore eyes!"—which is especially true for an Old English Sheepdog. Yup, there is nothing like knowing that your "best friend" is going to be waiting eagerly at the door EVERY time you open it. (Unless she is sprawled out sound asleep on your bed upstairs and doesn't hear the garage door open.)

On the other paw...er...hand, in the human realm, sometimes our greetings don't quite measure up to the Maggie model. Sometimes my fingers are glued to the keyboard and his are busy cutting mats or meeting a customer at the store. Well, that's ok because we know we'll be greeting each other across the table for dinner. Nowadays, this is our time to chat about the day and wind down. Now that we aren't running kids to dance class, the library, movies, etc., we take full advantage of this quiet time together.

Donna

Thanks, Angela, for the recent reminder about scherenschnitte. I got crazy into the craft one Christmas 12 years ago. Hunkered down at my kitchen table, I cut out patterns and snipped colored paper for eight or ten hours a day.

Lacy shreds were everywhere! And, judging by the numbness that plagued my cutting hand until the following spring, I clearly overdid the scherenschnitte. No matter! Creating eye-popping designs from unsuspecting sheets of paper was a right-brain joyride. The real thrill, though, was blessing a special, faraway friend with a one-of-a-kind gift.

In scherenschnitte, what you cut away is as important as what you leave in. The father of the prodigal understood that principle. He could have chided his son for being rebellious and squandering his fortune. Instead, he clipped away the parts of the conversation that would have served his own ego. The only thing left was pure, unadulterated love, the kind of love that heals us even when we "deserve" to be punished.

That's the kind of love I need to convey more often, even when numbness of heart obscures my priorities. Yes, it's the kind of love I can express more fluently the next time my neighbor's off-leash, 100-pound dog rushes toward my grocery-laden, stair-climbing figure.

Tammy

I aspire to be as good as a dog.

That's a sentiment I don't express every day...but it sure is true when it comes to this chapter. I don't even come close to measuring up to the kind of exuberant, loving greetings dogs give. I'm more like my cat (yes, my cat again). Sometimes I'm happy to see someone, sometimes I'm asleep or preoccupied with my own business, and sometimes (oh dear) I'm guilty of that haughty, "What do *you* want?" look.

Needless to say, I often forget how important something simple like a greeting can be. Yet when you greet someone, meeting their eyes and smiling, it's just surprising how much such a simple thing communicates. It really says, "I love you," and "I care about you," in a practical way.

Another fun story about greetings—at one of my previous jobs, I had a Korean coworker who was diligently trying to learn English after coming to this country. He was a very polite and pleasant man, and greeted me and the other employees with a polite "good morning" every day. I took the opportunity to ask him how to say "good morning" in Korean, and managed to remember that much at least. After that, when he said "Good morning" to me and the lady I worked with, we replied with "Jo-eun Ah-chim!" It always made him smile. (Probably at our pronunciation though!)

Shae

"Greet one another with a kiss of love" (1 Peter 5:14). My Gracie, a 10'-high Jack Russell yo-yo Terrier greets visitors at my door with a kiss of death! She is an absolutely precious angel most of the time but then metamorphoses into what vets call "protective fear mode," and I call "Pit Bull mode"; going for the back of a thigh, an ankle, or the hem of a coat if the victim is lucky. Woe to the unexpected FedEx guy or very courageous Jehovah Witness twosomes.

They say a dog and its master can develop similar quirks or tendencies—some owners even look like their dogs. I am happy, no, overjoyed to say that Grace and I look nothing alike thanks to waxing, and to my dear friend Leigh Valentine's "Non-Surgical Face Lift Kit." I do have self-protective gear though that kicks in around my enemies—those who have hurt me deeply, of whom there are one or two. Don't get me wrong—I don't snap. I just turn into an iceberg and go through the mechanics of being nice for the sake of.... GASP! It is time for me to pull back the surface for a deeper look at my heart. I expect I'll find a root of bitterness there. I wonder, is there such a thing as deliverance for dogs, too?

THAT KIND OF LOVE

Donna

Go ahead, ask me: "Donna, which part of unconditional love don't you understand?

Glad you asked. It's the *how-to* part (which, from where I sit, is unexplained in today's dare). Help me, ladies. I hit a brick wall reading this topic today. I know that God's kind of love is unconditional. The four of us and billions of others know that. But living it—that's the issue.

We sing, "I want to be more like You" because we *do*. Oh, yes! I want to be more like Christ. By His grace, I'm getting there—slowly, but surely. But there's a lot more road to hoe and I think it involves more than the *doing* of loving things.

Acts of love are good, helpful, and honoring to God and humankind. But I'm thinking unconditional love issues forth from a deeper well than that—a place of being loved so utterly and completely by Him that His very love becomes ours to give. After all, He loved us first.

Now, that's something I can hold on to! Please excuse me, ladies, as I retire to the soaking tub of His love.

Angela

The more I try to love unconditionally, the more I fall short. As a mother holding her innocent newborn, yes, unconditional love is what gushes from your heart. This darling who was nurtured from your body for nine months, this bundle of sweetness who wants only to be loved and hugged and fed by you—this child deserves nothing less than unconditional love. In my finite mind this is where unconditional love is made manifest—God's miracle of new life.

BUT when you meet people, marry people, work with people and FOR people, that initial bonding isn't there...and gee...like Donna I am baffled about the "how to" of it all.

Lord, help me to not only read First Corinthians 13 but to live it out daily.

Tammy

Ah, the big question with unconditional love: "How?"

Now mind you, I don't know either. I'm just trying and failing and hopefully improving. I did do one thing that seems to have helped. I asked God for His eyes so that anytime I look at a person, no matter how my heart is trying to disparage them, I can see them as His loved and specially created being.

Of course, my heart usually doesn't follow along. My heart asks, "*This* person? But there's nothing good about them!" Yet somehow, once I've remembered how God sees them, my own vision of them is changed. I may not understand it fully in my mind—I can't see the depths of their heart and understand everything that God sees in them—but it still has a powerful impact.

God's eyes help me see them as a precious person with a unique destiny and potential only He knows about. Asking God for His eyes has helped me a lot.

Of course, I may very well need to turn around and get God's eyes back in my head again the very next second, but that's the nice thing about Him—if you really ask Him for something and keep pursuing it, He turns up to fulfill your request time and time again.

Shae

"I love you, period." What an incredible use of a tiny dot for raising the value quotient of love! Who knew how transformational a period could be? LOL.

Unconditional love is what we need in this binge/purge world of bulimic love. I recall a friend of mine in her early sixties, a beautiful woman, drop dead gorgeous inside and out. After 40+ years of marriage, her husband told her he wanted a divorce. The reason? A 25-year-old "hottie."

We have become a throwaway society, even in love! We lack intangibles that make life most meaningful especially genuine love, which we all need but that our materialistic fleshly society makes it very hard to find. Only when I emptied myself fully could I fill myself up, and in turn be an outflow of the agape well of love that people would find. Donna so beautifully and wisely described the well as a "place of being loved so utterly and completely by Him that His very love becomes ours to give."

The unconditional love of God shown to me by family, friends, and perfect strangers is the reason why I have moved beyond many heartbreaks and heartaches, sorrows and dark times. Because of their outflow of love, I do not look back on those trials with regret or remorse, but as tremendous gifts of love in its purest form.

PART II

*Love and Impossible
Possibilities*

PROFOUND MYSTERY

Tammy

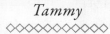

I have to admit, when it comes to understanding this chapter on cherishing your spouse, I have to borrow Paul's words: "This is a profound mystery" (Eph. 5:32). Honestly, I've never experienced anything like this—being so united that your spouse's body is your own and their victories and defeats are your own. I have no idea what that feels like.

I just thank the Lord for this amazing earthly miniature image of His own nature, and I'm rooting for all you married folks as you daily live out such a holy thing.

Donna

Ditto, Tammy. Cherishing and being cherished in that kind of union sounds like Heaven on earth, which I imagine (as much as I am able) that it would be. Quite a stretch to visualize such bliss, isn't it? Kind of like trying to imagine how life in Heaven plays out: How does it feel to enjoy uninterrupted physical well-being? What is it like to experience no ebb of joy? What does it mean to relate to our Creator in the absolute absence of distraction?

Oh, how this imperfect piece of creation groans! Not that I imagine flawlessness in any union of humans. I may be a dreamer, but I'm not delusional. Yet, being an habitual people-watcher (isn't that what writers do?), I've witnessed from afar moments of marital bliss. I've written them on the hard drive of my heart...sweet reminders of what can be.

Sure, I recognize that any reflection of God's glory is housed in earthen vessels. There always a crack in the pot. But, hey, on this side of Heaven, that kind of imperfection looks terrific to me!

Shae

Have you ever had a vanilla sundae with the works—the whipped cream, hot rich fudge, crushed peanuts, oozing caramel, Oreo crumbs, and of course, the cherry? If you have, you will understand what I mean by, "Love goes so much better with cherish!" It really does.

In my previous marriage we lacked this extension of love and I know the deprivation contributed to the demise of our relationship. How I longed for what today's lesson dares us to do for our loved one—those little but by no means inconsequential things we do by choice, because we want to, not because we're asked or because we have to, just because he or she is the most precious treasure on the face of the earth!

There is much truth in this teaching. When my husband stopped cherishing me, I felt tossed to the wind, dismissed, and disjointed—the fabric of our relationship unraveled. He preferred to put his energy and time into something else—not work-related. The void—oh my, it was so painful! How I missed our heart-to-heart talks and hand-in-hand times. Bewildered, hurt, I wondered, *what is wrong with me...don't I excite him anymore...has he fallen out of love with me...I'm a horrible wife*. It is amazing how downcast my spirit was and how mechanical love became when "cherish" vanished. In hindsight, I see areas of opportunity to cherish that I missed in that relationship, and I am determined not to fall short in this one.

You Win!

Angela

When we had our home built 20 years ago, I had pictured in my mind exactly which windows went where, what doors opened into which room, how the porch would look, where the stairs and bathrooms would be placed, and how the kitchen would be arranged. I had heard horror stories from others about how stressful and traumatic it was to have a house built, so I was apprehensive, yet excited.

It turned out to be one of the most fun times in my life. I was used to creating paintings, sweaters, meals, dance costumes, articles, and stories...now I was creating a home sweet home—our home. I must admit I appreciate every nook and cranny of our home and when we left it for three years to live in Hawaii, I missed it.

The reason my story has a happy ending is because my husband let me "win" concerning the decorating and cosmetic aspects of the house, and I let him "win" regarding the plumbing, electrical, and man-interesting side of stuff.

Everyone likes to win and feel like a winner—keeping each other in the winner's circle by seriously thinking about what is really important to you and letting the other things go makes (to use an overused term) a win-win marriage!

Donna
◇◇◇◇◇◇◇◇◇◇

Speaking of couples and houses, I remember my parents hiring a carpenter to finish our above-ground basement. I was ten and thought people who hired carpenters to finish their basements were rich. You can imagine how close to the floor my chin dragged when, even after the work was completed, my allowance failed to budge.

Surely my depression-era parents would have preferred to save a few Benjamins by remodeling the basement themselves. However, my dad was more intellect than handyman. Solomon himself would have recommended delegating the job to a professional.

Yet no sooner had the carpenter packed up his table saw than Dad decided to add his own touch to the remodel. Why not drill through 12 inches of concrete foundation and install a window in the otherwise perfectly-finished bathroom?

My mother's eyebrows met her hairline at the thought. After

all, when Dad tried using a screwdriver to chip ice off the freezer (*why,* Dad?), he punched a hole clear through the Freon line. Expecting the Frigidaire to blow up, we all ran out to the front stoop.

Despite her reservations, Mom let Dad win. I think it did him a world of good to be trusted that way. He did a fine job, too. More than four decades later, the house is still standing, window and all!

Shae

...and the moral of this chapter is "Don't let your husband move you into a house only 80% complete—it will NEVER get done!" LOL, but I won't even go there. Well, maybe for a nano second.

How often I had to resist the eye roll. You know what I mean, right? When you know for sure that you are right (no, really, you have proof), and you are looking at him wondering what vegetable group he belongs to.

Pride got in the way-eth far too often-eth, especially when the sky really wouldn't have fallen in had I let him win. In my quests for the adrenaline high of being right at times and in not becoming a doormat that always acquiesced, I would sometimes come out with my guns blasting for that release of speaking my mind and having it heard; but he often did the same. Then it was a case of pride and the clash of two people who once worked as a unit that were now separate, and it caused fragility to the point of snap—no graceful bending as the author pointed out with the example of the palm tree by the ocean.

I have since discovered a delicious treasure in being willing to let the other win—it is called "humble pie," and it sometimes has yummy consequences.

Tammy

This may be one of the bigger reasons I don't have any interest in getting married.

Don't get me wrong, I think marriage is great. I admire those who make their marriages lasting and beautiful, and I'm always happy for my friends as they make this commitment. (20-somethings—it's the matrimonial age!) Still, it's just never been something I want for myself.

Me, I like my independence I guess. I like deciding for myself, and not having to contend with another person's opinion. I like being able to say, "Japanese food tonight," or "I'm going back to school again," or "I think I'll move over there," without having to consult with someone else, and maybe end up giving in to what they want, or making accommodations for them instead. I have to admit, I like the single life.

I sure do admire married people who can handle this aspect of their relationship, though.

No Hitting Below the Belt

Angela

In my opinion, setting up some rules is an excellent idea for newlyweds. When the blush fades from the honeymoon high and the dirty dishes are stacked high in the sink, these guidelines will keep the battles from becoming too bloody—emotionally, mentally, and/or physically.

I remember two violent clashes (not physical), and they still cause me heart pain. Only by the grace of God did we triumph through those times. For us, there came a time when we just stopped talking, talking, talking about a subject that we were never going to agree on, and agreed to disagree.

Eventually we realized that silence really is golden and after awhile most of what anyone argues about is trivial.

Shae

I hear you Angela. To extend that quote, "Silence is golden, let's all shut up and get rich quick." This doesn't mean side-stepping controversial or difficult issues—just thinking before speaking. Words can have a wonderful effect on a relationship but oh my, when flung like mud to expose another's shortcomings or failings, they can cause permanent stains that no amount of Tide Extra with Bleach can get out, except by the grace and ability of God to heal deep hurts.

I recall a time in a moment of anger when someone dredged up what I had spoken in confidence and trust, then embellished those things and hurled them at me cruelly, and in front of other loved ones, to boot. Trust died that day a horrible death and it took a long time before I could entrust anyone—even God—with delicate confidences.

I know there have been times in anger when I have been a basket mouth—emptying stuff in the heat of argument that I shouldn't have. There were times too that I read back things that I really should have written in the sand to be erased by winds of love and mercy rather than in indelible ink on paper that lasts forever and can be read over and over.

The good news is, I have learned how to wire my jaw, and that guardrail is a *good thang.*

Donna

"Love helps you...to set up guardrails in your relationship." That sounds like good advice all around, because boundaries take a fair amount of the guesswork out of conflict.

After moving to Colorado from New York, a friend from my home state came to visit. I showed her around the Rockies and took her to the top of Pike's Peak. What an amazing place: topaz skies border clay-colored soil; breathtaking vistas suck out what precious little oxygen you manage to suck in.

Oh, and did I mention, *no guardrails?* No kidding, you drive around hairpin turns on unpaved roads with nothing between you and 12,000 feet of freefall. When an overly-confident, lead-footed tourist made a steep right turn on his descent, he lost control of his car and slid straight toward us, nearly knocking us off the mountain. "Jesus!" my friend and I shouted.

No impact. My guest and I were safe. There were still a couple of feet between us and The Edge.

That's when the guardrail of my heart came down. "Moron!" I shouted, my body shaking. "You could have killed us!" That wasn't fair. The poor guy didn't need me to rip his head off. He was probably kicking himself already. Besides, he wasn't a killer, just a bad driver.

Oh, and I did I mention, *really bad?*

Tammy

I am so grateful for the way my parents implemented guardrails in their relationship...and in their fights. I never saw them argue as a child, and I can't begin to say what a huge difference that made. They never fought physically and they *never* mentioned divorce—it wasn't an option, right from day one.

As a result, I had a home life growing up that was (while not perfect) beautifully peaceful and luxurious when compared with many of my peers. I remember one time in middle school talking to some kids at lunch. I must have said something along the lines of, "My parents would never get divorced." To them, this only meant that I couldn't imagine it, but their cross-examining made it clear that they "knew much better"—*anybody* could get divorced, in their minds. But in mine, it wasn't an option because it had never been one for my parents. Even after all their doubt-mongering, I was still certain that it would never happen.

And it never has. The guardrails are still sturdy, thank the good Lord.

SLEEP-OVERS AND PIKE'S PEAK

Angela

Remembering what makes each other smile keeps our marriage fresh. In the middle of a Pennsylvania snow, we talk about the flock of lime-green parrots that flew past our condo's open lanai in Honolulu. During a quiet evening, we talk about how noisy and nosey the little girls were who came for sleep-overs with our daughters. When eating at our favorite restaurant (Ruth's Chris), we talk about eating soup and hotdogs in early lean years. And he has a knack of nick-naming people—family, neighbors, coworkers, politicians—that always brings a chuckle.

We choose to treasure the good memories, the current fun experiences, and look forward to treasuring exciting new adventures.

Donna

Years before we drove to the summit of Pike's Peak, my good friend and I represented our school at a conference for educators. For teacher-bookworm-learning-geeks, it was heaven. So, when we had a free night midway through the convention, what did we do? What else? Had dinner, retired to our hotel room, put on our PJs, and *read*.

Among our accumulated treasures was a gift-mix test that rates motivational tendencies. We sharpened our pencils and took the test. When we tabulated our individual results, we exclaimed geekily, "Wow, we really *are* twins separated at birth!"

Both of us had strong inclinations toward teaching. That's handy; after all, she was the principal and I was teaching English and math. There were other common strengths and—yes—a shared weakness. We were black-and-white, cut-and-dried, not-by-inclination-merciful types. We were... uh...prone to be disapproving of others.

Wait—before you disapprove us, let me remind you that, according to *The Love Dare,* we were just being human...woefully human.

On the upside, we *have* mellowed since those days. (Whew!)

Tammy

Angela, yours certainly does sound like a *delightful* marriage! I would say "Lucky you," but I think "Blessed are you" is probably more correct, yes? ^_^

This chapter certainly points to the importance of the "little things" in life and in a relationship. Even the simplest joys can be multiplied so much, simply by having another person there, sharing in that joy with you. I've also noticed that sometimes, being reminded of something I used to enjoy by someone who shared that with me can rekindle an enjoyment that had faded into the dusty corners of my memory.

Little pleasures like pretty seashells on the beach, hot tomato soup on a cold day, or new favorite shoes—whether discovered or rediscovered—sharing them with another person makes them twice as wonderful, every time.

Can of Worms Alert

Tammy

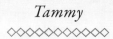

It strikes me as more than a little bit shocking how casually some people take this charge to honor their spouse. I'll be honest—for a single person, it puts me off to the whole marriage idea when I hear someone telling unkind jokes about their husband or wife.

I'm talking about something I see in group settings many times. I am sure it starts as simple teasing, a way to relate to the other married people: "Oh your spouse does *that?* Let me tell you how much worse *mine* is." Sometimes it's nothing too important or mean, but other times I am surprised by how hurtful these comments to others can become. All I can say is, *that* is not honoring.

It's so much more honorable to spread good things about your spouse. Why is it so easy to get into little conversational competitions about whose spouse is worse, rather than whose is better, more thoughtful, more sweet and attentive, more generous, et cetera? Granted, I sometimes do hear people "bragging" on their spouses in a much more honorable way, but sometimes it just doesn't seem like it happens enough.

I feel like I shouldn't preach on this point, not being one who can live my own lesson (in my non-existent marriage), but can I at least make a request? To all married people, on behalf of the single people listening to you: please practice honor in your speech about your spouse, and don't discourage us.

Donna

Can of worms alert! There are two groups of people whose opinions about family and marital matters are widely unappreciated: the childless and the never married. (Oh joy! I'm in both groups. The good news is, I'll never need an upper lip wax. The bad news is that wearing duct tape across my mouth does not enhance my chances of finding a mate.)

We childless wonders needn't tell people how to raise their kids. And I agree with Tammy, since we singles haven't walked in the moccasins of the married, we lack a credible platform from which to preach about marital honor.

Which explains the third reason I go through duct tape like water: over the years, I've witnessed so many friends and acquaintances being (routinely) dismissive of their husbands. It's embarrassing, and tempts a rebuke to the tip of my Brooklyn-born tongue.

I'd like to think that, given the chance, I would appreciate and honor my husband. Then again, I was pretty sure I'd resist that chocolate mug cake tonight.

Please pass the duct tape.

Shae

Sorry to burst your bubble Donna, but the upper lip wax is a given married or not after oh, say 45—as is the chin wax—unless you plan to sweep your patio with your face by the time you are 60...lol. Then again, duct tape might just work!

It is said, "Pull a whisker from a cat; get a claw mark on your back. Pull a whisker from a man, turn and run as fast as you can. Pull a whisker from your wife, pray to the Lord there's an afterlife." Woe to he who makes any mention of bearded women, porcupines, or nanny goats when I am around. Love me, love (and honor) my chin whisker, I always say. Tammy, Kitty will relate.

Sigh...mid-life is a season where honor has to be at its peak—in my books. Someone pass the Nair please. I know I can't take my tweezers with me when I die, but I'm going to ask God anyhow.

Angela

◇◇◇◇◇◇◇◇◇◇

Wow—guilty as charged. Way too many times I have mentioned some "unadoring" qualities of my husband to a trusted friend… never at a party or in a crowd (probably because I shy away from groups of more than 4 or 5, except, of course on one of my favorite elbow-sharpened days of the year—Black Friday).

Reading what you thought was very convicting, and I appreciate your perspectives as unmarrieds. After 31 years of living in the forest, I need to remember what a strong and enduring tree I have right beside me…sheltering this squirrelly nut case.

It is much easier to concentrate on each other now than during our child-raising years when life was so "reactive" rather than "proactive." Soccer games, horseback riding lessons, art classes, dance recitals, book reports, math that boggled my mind beyond belief (thank goodness for Daddy), and all the trauma that teenage hormones could conjure up left us drained empty as we kissed our pillows goodnight.

Both seasons of life are very special—the trick is appreciating and enjoying whatever season God has gifted you with at the time.

TICK TOCKER

Angela

For the first ten years of our marriage I just didn't "get it." As a confirmed control freak I assumed that my guy would see life exactly the way I saw it—perfectly clear and organized. For ten years I was practicing the definition of insanity—doing the same thing over and over and expecting different results.

I followed my parent's Ozzie and Harriet, June and Ward (minus the pearls) examples and assumed this was life worldwide. Dinner on the table at 5 each evening. Sunday was for going to church, dressed in our "church clothes." Saturday was grocery day, Tuesday was laundry day...you get the picture.

When it came to the "Sunday was for going to church" part, hubby just wasn't into it. Although he belonged to a mainline denomination church and we were married in a church, for years he didn't go with me. Finally, after years of whining and griping to him every Sunday morning while I got the girls dressed, I decided to stop hounding him and just pray. Pray I did, for the next several years.

Then one Sunday we started going to a very small non-denomination church near our home. The people were nice and their hugs welcoming. We learned a lot about a personal relationship with Jesus there—and I learned about the life-changing power of prayer.

Tammy

Isn't it funny how we can go before the Lord, praying our hearts out for a person—for something we have in mind for them—and eventually come out changed ourselves? Not that the things we pray for are wrong, or that we were the ones who needed to be changed in whatever the situation was. Perhaps it's just the time in His presence—we go there for someone else, and can't help being enriched, refreshed, and matured by His touch.

That alone seems to me to be a perfect excuse to find time to pray for anyone and everyone. ^_^

Shae

There is nothing more beautiful in a marriage than a praying husband and wife. Genuinely seeking the Lord in prayer should be the number one method in problem solving, in getting off the treadmill of conflict, in renewing the romantic spark, and reigniting it. I could not change my husband, but I could have made the decision to change myself—choosing to become a determined intercessor for my husband—for our relationship. Praying for him may have given me an extreme makeover in the process.

If I could do it over again, there would be much more time spent praying for healing, for the order of God in my household, for new beginnings, and for restoration of our love. I now know that a praying woman can literally transform the atmosphere in her home. When our hearts beat in harmony with the heart of God, He will surpass our expectations when we cry out to Him. Prayer helps us feel His burden, and He hears us and answers us—oh so profoundly. The Psalmist knew this and said that those who sow in tears, who go out weeping, carrying seed to sow will reap and return with songs of joy, carrying sheaves with him (see Ps. 126:5-6). I want sheaves!

Donna

As I read Angela's wisdom, I thought, *You definitely can't commit the sin of changing thy spouse if you don't have one.* Yet, we singles don't get a pass on this issue. Truth be told, you can spend a lot of energy imagining a mate so perfect, he or she who wouldn't need changing. It's the same game of insanity some married people play, but this one's in the *Wii* version.

Oooohhh...creepy. Not that I haven't played a round...or

ten. But, by the grace of God, I'm smart enough now (OK, old enough)—to know that concocting the perfect "virtual" mate can cloud your vision for the real thing. In fact, my pastor preached just this Sunday about having such an over-developed wish list (spouse-wise) that if God hand-delivered to your doorstep His idea of your better half, you'd kick the poor soul to the curb. (That's the Brooklyn version of what my pastor said.)

Which reminds me...back when my biological clock was still ticking, I was taught to intercede for my future (and un-known) spouse—for His walk with God, for wisdom, pro-tection, etc. I did that for years. Hmmm...I wonder when and why I stopped...

UNDER THE COVERS

Angela

In my opinion, relationships and marriages are as different as snowflakes, fingerprints, flavors of ice cream. What works for one couple may not work for another.

Being intimate with your spouse is not like being intimate with your heavenly Father or your children...or your pet, for that matter. Intimacy is a process that takes time and patience. It isn't just talking about your likes and dislikes at the moment. Intimacy is wanting to know what keeps him awake at night, what makes him happy, what words encourage him, what motivates him, what he dreams about, what matters most to him—these things are worth watching for and tucking away in the recesses of your heart and mind. Love makes you want to be more intimate.

Donna

Being intimate with God is, arguably, easier than being intimate with anyone else, if only because His love is so unadulterated, so unconditional, so without the machinations that complicate human relationships.

One of the purest moments of intimacy I've ever experienced occurred one night long ago when I was at my lowest ebb, physically speaking. I was midway through a five-month barrage of chemotherapy and I was a sight—pale as a sheet with a pea-green cast, bald as a bowling ball, and weak as water.

I was the dullest of company, certainly not what the world would have labeled "a catch." But the Lover of my soul didn't seem to mind. Instead, He chose my worst moment to "come calling." As I awaited the reassuring light of dawn (the light which shouted, "Hallelujah! You made it!"), He made His tender presence known. It was a moment so intimate and tangible I turned my head as if to see Him standing there.

No. I couldn't see Him with my eyes, but He was there all right. Without a doubt, He was there.

Tammy

I have a question. Maybe it will sound naïve, and maybe it doesn't have an answer other than the final recourse we all resort to after chatting with a "why-wondering" three-year-old for long enough: "Because!" Maybe that's the best answer here, but I still want to throw this out there.

We all have a longing for intimacy—I certainly agree. And God knows every one of us better than anyone else ever can. No doubt about that either; He knows us with the most complete intimacy. Why, then, do so many people seem to need human intimacy? Particularly those who know God—why look any further?

I guess I can understand why a person who doesn't know God would feel that way. I think, if I didn't know Him, I would really, really want to get married; I'd be seeking that intimacy as much as possible. As it is, though, I already have the most intimate relationship. Personally, I don't feel a need for anything else.

I realize, of course, that I am a statistical minority. So I guess my question is: why do/did *you* want to get married?

Shae

Donna, you brought tears to my eyes. Isn't it wonderful when He shows up in our darkness. Did you feel healing in His presence? I did. Tammy, to answer your question, I desired marriage again because of an encounter with Love Himself.

Several years ago when I thought I could never love again, Jesus appeared to me in a dream. We sat across from one another at a table, much like two lovers would, and He gazed into my eyes. His eyes were soft with a glint of tears and sparkled in the light of His very presence. They had compassion in them, the likes I had never ever experienced, and they were of a color I cannot even describe. His smile was warm and inviting, and His lips—the sweetest lips, because on them were the most amazing words of tenderness as He professed His love for me. He took my hands, and drew me unto Himself, and whispered love words, but words weren't even necessary, because everything He told me, He had already spoken with His eyes. His voice had a gentle rhythm, a soothing lilt that sounded like a crooner's love song that played endlessly in my spirit.

Love had not eluded me after all. With such profound, intimate love in my spirit—I had to pour it out on someone!

HOMEWORK

Shae

This teaching encourages us to study our mate, to engage in a lifelong journey of knowing one another better. I appreciate the fact that the authors also stress the importance of understanding and wisdom.

While in our dating phase, "Bob," my ex-husband and I spent hours and hours gleaning knowledge of each other, talking about childhoods, struggles, fears, hopes, and dreams. As trust mounted, we felt comfortable exposing our weaknesses, feeling less vulnerable as we grew in love.

That pack of facts that we both held of each other could either make or break the relationship—the presence or lack of understanding and wisdom would determine the outcome. *Understanding* lifts the meaning from the knowledge we glean and *wisdom* knows what to do with the facts next. Sadly, the lack of true understanding and wisdom turned some of that knowledge into assault weapons—and the relationship unraveled like a poorly knit sweater until at last we were two separate threads.

Angela

The more intimate with your mate, the more you understand your mate. Taking the time to appreciate why he thinks and acts the way he does keeps misunderstandings at a minimum. For instance, I married a workaholic career military guy who traveled a lot and a country boy raised inland. Rather than forego coveted summer vacations to the beach, I adapted and drove the girls and I to Disney World (16 hours!) and other various beaches over the years; we also flew husbandless to Barbados and Hawaii. Knowing hubby would have been miserable with sand between his toes, we opted for some quality mommy-daughters sun in the fun time...and had even more fun telling him tales after returning home sweet home.

This set-up would not work for everyone, but it did for us. Understanding each other is key for a lasting relationship of love.

Donna

How precious, Angela, that husband and wife can learn to "make room" for one another! A loving marriage like yours requires an intense commitment to lifelong learning—about one another and about *self*.

A passion for lifelong learning is part of what landed me in Bible college when I was uh…40-something. On dorm move-in day, I was surrounded by mostly 20-somethings and three other clearly-crazy-but-mature women like me. I assumed I would be assigned quarters with the older crowd. Instead, I was asked to bunk with a 19-year-old. She was a sweetheart, but we had *nothing* in common.

It's not as though I was uncomfortable with young people; I'd just completed six years teaching high school and enjoyed interacting with youth. But, each evening, Miss Scuderi and her plan book retreated to a teen-less cave. In the dorm, there would be no retreat. The only option? Surrender.

Which was exactly what *The* Doctor ordered. Rooming with Gretel was wonderfully life-changing. As Carl Jung said: "The meeting of two personalities is like the contact of two chemical substances: if there is any reaction, both are transformed."

Tammy

◇◇◇◇◇◇◇◇◇◇◇

When it comes to making a lifelong study of another person, I look to my parents again as the nearest scholarly experts. They've been deepening their understanding of each other for 26 years, and it's still the cutest thing to see when they find out something new about each other—like when my dad finally realized that my mom doesn't eat mustard. (Somehow, in over two decades, it just hadn't come up in a way that brought his attention to it, mustard fanatic that he is.)

Of course, mustard isn't a big deal, and so they didn't make a big deal out of it. Dad just kind of looked at Mom and said, "I didn't know you don't like mustard," to which she merely responded with another confirmation of her preference. But the look on his face was adorable; I can only describe it as a surprised expression that seemed to say, "Well! Aren't *you* the most interesting mystery I've known for years?"

I think they are both still pretty interested in their field of study. ^_^

Possibly Impossible

Shae

The Love Dare starts with a secret and this chapter reveals it; that we cannot manufacture unconditional (agape) love out of our own hearts. I agree wholeheartedly. The lack of agape love in my marriage created irreparable distance.

Shhh. My husband's bothersome habits so annoyed me at times, I actually withheld love. Then he'd focus on my short-comings and faults and shut me out. Ouch-Chihuahua. Although we lived in the same home, slept in the same bed, we lived in the Great Divide.

I have since learned, via a personal, exquisite, intimate relationship with God, that love goes way beyond feelings. It is in fact deliberate; something couples have to decide to give and to show; a choice to demonstrate love to one another in every circumstance. God showed humankind agape love by revealing Himself through a human body. Emmanuel. God came near. He sympathized with our weaknesses, was approachable, and people came to Him in droves. Not one person who encountered Jesus feared rejection. He bridged their shortcomings with His love. Without His love touch, I would still be creating distance in my relationships. Now that Jesus has built the bridge, I am able to love so much better.

Angela

I know for a fact that I would not have a 31-year marriage if not for God Almighty's ability for impossible love. When troubles over finances or children discipline problems would arise, only knowing that God was ultimately in control kept me from completely losing control (of my mind). Knowing that God is the Solver of all problems gave me the strength and peace of mind to forge ahead into the depths of family life and love.

With God *all* things are possible.

Donna

All things are possible with God, but the learning curve is steep at times. I remember the night I finally learned to love my dad for real—terribly imperfectly, but genuinely, not because he was my father, but because *he was.*

My dad and I did not have an easy relationship. It grew no easier with time. One night after Dad's dementia had become undeniable, he and I sat in his living room. He watched TV; I folded towels. I found myself staring at him as he gazed unself-consciously through the flickering blue haze, his eyes fixed on the television screen.

In a revelatory instant, both the impossibility of love and its irresistible nature were clear. The things I found challenging about Dad were the areas that most closely mirrored my own imperfections. My love for both of us was impaired!

Just as I thought my heart would break under the crushing weight of regret, a wave of God's love washed over me. I saw Dad differently, as though through God's eyes and not my own.

The impossible made irresistible.

Tammy

As much as I don't like to hear, "You *can't* do this," I have no argument with the plain fact that I can't love unconditionally—that *agape* love is truly impossible for me. I think, after coming this far into the book, and reading about all these facets of love, as well as examining my own weak, human heart, there just isn't any way I can deny it.

Perfect love *must* come from God. And, though salvation starts it all, it's never a "one dose for life" vaccination. God's love is something you have to "take daily, with food and drink." You have to get it inside you every single day until it pours out of you into your relationships. When you get that way, you can spread the healing medication of His love easier than the common cold.

JESUS LOVES ME

Angela

I can't even imagine the depth of love that Jesus has for me—for all people. When I watched the movie *The Passion* by Mel Gibson, the soul-deep anguish that tore at my heart and spirit was almost unbearable. I watched Him carry the cross, saw His mother's despair, heard the people mocking Him, and turned my eyes away from the beatings and the nails piercing His body. This is love. Jesus is love. The Bible is full of God's love for His children.

His death is my life. I comprehend this oxymoron on faith alone. He is the beginning and the end of all I ever need to know.

Donna

"Nor can love like this be earned." That's for sure. Ask anyone who's received it in spite of themselves (that would be everybody who's received it, including me).

Apparently, there is no edge too rough or attitude too cynical; Jesus gave His all anyway—all that I lacked and everything I or anyone else could ever need.

Talk about the *perfect* gift.

Tammy

I remember meeting Jesus Christ about eight years ago, and I remember how, for me, it was like love didn't exist until then. Whatever measure of it I'd scraped together from the world just evaporated in the sunshine of that first love—the face of Jesus. There's no one like Him, and there's nothing like the change He brings into every corner of life, relationships of all kinds included.

He's the beginning and the end of all love, and you just can't talk about love without Him.

Shae

How right you are Tammy, and how spot on this chapter's thought that His love made the greatest sacrifice to meet our greatest need.

"What are you looking for?" This is the question Jesus asked of two of His disciples, Andrew and John, and that He asks of every human heart. I answered with what my heart yearned for the most, which really wasn't for a "what" but for a "Whom."

"I am looking for a faith in which I can call myself beautiful and believe it. For someone who would know me from the inside out, someone who could hear the longings of my heart for the type of peace and joy that sings, that scars. I am looking for a future like no other because of blazing love. I am searching for a fulfillment I have no words for."

Those things I could not find in the world: not in a store, in a jar of miracle cream, not from family, friends, the church, or even in a marriage.

Jesus' reply of 2,000 years ago echoed in my spirit, "Come and see." I found all of my yearnings fulfilled in that "come and see" place, the very heart of Perfect Love Himself. In searching for love I discovered that Love had already called my name.

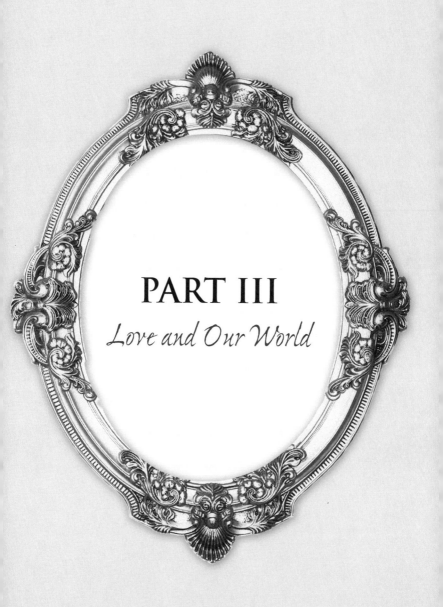

PART III

Love and Our World

SEPTEMBER 11, 2001

Angela

One fact of life that has proven true for me over the years—people will always let you down. Putting total faith in your spouse, children, friend, teacher, preacher, boss, mentor, or your manicurist is asking for hurt, disappointment, and disillusionment.

God is the only One who can be there for you always and forever. He was with me when Mom died of a sudden heart attack while she was reading her Bible sitting in her favorite chair in the living room. He was with me when I sat alone on the floor in our Honolulu condo watching the second World Trade Tower crash to the ground and the Pentagon explode in flames—with my husband on business in Washington and our daughter in college in Manhattan.

In my mind's eye that day I saw Jesus slowly walking through the rubble, His robe stirring the ashes of things and people. He was so very sad. But He was there. He is always with us—forever and ever.

Donna
◇◇◇◇◇◇◇◇◇◇◇

Jesus in the rubble of September 11, 2001. Quintessential grace meets the ultimate bad day.

September 11th ended differently than it began. The smothering humidity of previous days had lifted, giving way to the bluest of skies and a spring in the step of New Yorkers. All that changed—quickly. Bad days are wired that way. They enter the frame without fanfare and unleash their fury without warning. Up is down. Left is right. Nothing is what it seemed to be.

Not all of life's surprises transpire in a moment; some of them sneak up on you. Maybe you woke up married and went to bed divorced. The warning signs were there but, until the papers were signed, you held out hope.

I remember "waking up" to the reality that I would never have children. I was 40-ish and single...you do the math. It was a moment of truth and all I could say was, "How'd I end up here?"

How thankful I am that, in time, I reached a place of utter satisfaction in *His* love. Will I ever marry? Maybe, but not because I feel alone.

Tammy

Wow, Donna. I can hardly imagine facing a realization like that, and the struggle it must have been. (I am assuming you had expected to have children, of course.) I can only admire your strength and maturity to have satisfied yourself with the Lord, even when faced with other longings being denied.

I truly hope, if I faced something similar, that I'd be able to continue to be fully satisfied with only Him. Right now I think I am, but then I never wanted marriage or children in the first place, so I feel like I haven't been tested—I haven't sacrificed something I wanted and come out content.

I'd like to think I would continue to be satisfied with Him, even if I was denied something I wanted. I certainly pray for His grace to make that possible.

Shae

His grace is like a flowing fountain, Tammy. We can tap in anytime.

What struck me the most was: "His Holy Spirit is renewing your heart." Thank goodness for all of our sakes. Sending us the Holy Spirit as our Helper and Holy Companion was one of the most wonderful things Jesus did. When I accepted Jesus, God breathed on me and His Spirit entered my heart and life. The Holy Spirit brought me the unconditional love of

God and calmly reassured me through every extreme I have encountered, including the death of my precious mother in a fire, and divorce, that He would be here to help me and satisfy my needs. Although I cannot see Him because He is God's Spirit, I see evidence every day of His presence in my life. Just as leaves carried by the wind are proof that a breeze is blowing, so is the fact that I am able to love confirmation that the Holy Spirit is touching my life. His is a never-ending fountain of love that quenches my desperate thirst moment-by-moment. The promise of God that I have immersed myself in for the day is:

"I love them that love Me; and those that seek Me early shall find Me" (Proverbs 8:17 KJV).

Because of this incredible relationship, I know the reality of Romans 5:5, the love of God shed abroad in my heart by the Holy Ghost!

YOU MOVED

Angela

◇◇◇◇◇◇◇◇◇

Reading today's chapter reminded me of a story about a young couple back in the day before seatbelt laws. The girl sat very close to her beau while he was driving his convertible. They were inseparable and had permanent smiley faces. Over the years they married, had children, had an empty nest, and had a conversation. "Honey, remember back when we were so in love and we sat really close together when you were driving?"

"Yes, I remember."

"What happened?"

"Well, I'm still in the same seat behind the wheel. You moved."

That's the way my relationship sometimes is with the Lord.

He is faithful to be in the same place, directing my path to fulfilling my destiny; but I move away from Him because I'm too busy, too selfish, or too distracted. Every so often I stop for a moment and purposefully move back across the seat to snuggle up beside my First Love.

Donna
◇◇◇◇◇◇◇◇◇◇◇

Baby-boomer recess at P.S. 153. Tommy runs as far from Suzie as the schoolyard fence allows yelling, "You've got cooties!"

A manly man in Buster Browns and a clip-on tie, Tommy exclaims to his buddies, "I hate girls!" Yeah, and my name is Wonder Woman. Soon as I land my invisible airplane, I'll unleash my Lasso of Truth on you.

Not to mix metaphors, but we humans are funny ducks—we quack out of both sides of our beaks. We want attention, but pretend to avoid it. We want love, but prize our independence. We find unspeakable joy in God's presence and find silly reasons to be unavailable.

Mea culpa! There are days when I allow the Distractions of the Unbelievably Unimportant to steal my fellowship with Him...days when I allow the chirp of an incoming email to draw me away from our secret place to the farthest end of my apartment. How urgent could an email possibly be? I live in Colorado, but not under Cheyenne Mountain. NORAD's got that handled.

Yes, I "have rejected Him in many ways...yet He still loves" me, cooties and all.

Tammy

I love the story of Hosea. It's perfectly wonderful knowing you are on the receiving end of love like that. It's much more challenging to actually live out the giving end of a relationship, particularly one that becomes very one-way in terms of the demonstrations of love. I regret that I must admit to having taken the easier way out in the past—"cut my losses" and run from a friend. To this day, I'm sorry for it.

At the same time, however, it's hard to know when to hang on and when to let go in a friendship. (I'm mostly talking about friendships, because that's what I know.) When do you sacrifice for that friend, and when do you let go, realizing that the relationship is just dragging you endlessly down? Or is that even an option? Would God always want us to continue to give, even to a friend who is destroying us?

All I know is we need to pray for wisdom as we struggle to imitate His faithfulness.

Shae

Love Hosea and I am also a fan of Jonah! The same Love that pursued him with the ravaging sea and the stinky belly of the great fish cried out to me with a storm. Notice I said "with"!

God has never left or forsaken me but I have sometimes distanced myself from Him. My turning point came on the day that my son and I ran from our home with nothing more in tow than Mr. Bear, our Bible, and my purse. Later that evening, I finally came to grips with grace and promised my Father that I would always draw near to Him.

My storm was His cry—God wanted me back. What possessed Him to welcome me back when I turned my back on Him? Love. Love possessed Him. The same love that pursued Jonah caused me to cry out, "O, help me God!"

When I knocked again on God's heart asking for His presence, He opened it not an inch, but wide open, not because of what was in my heart, but because of what is in His. This is our Faithful Pursuer. His love is so great that His cry was in the taking down of my heart with labor to bring me back.

Jonah said, "I was in this condition...and yet..." "And yet" is God's unconditional, relentless, and faithful love in my life.

ZOOT SUITS OF ARMOR

Angela

People—especially Christians—face more temptations today than in any time in history. The Internet exposes people of all ages to sights and concepts that have warped and perverted even the most sacred of institutions—marriage.

One moment, please, while I step up on my soapbox. Christians are tempted to accept the "tolerance" ploy and disregard the clear tenets in the Bible. Christians are tempted to go along with redefining marriage for the sake of being accepting. Yes, of course, Christians are supposed to love and accept and be tolerant...but we should not condone people's actions that are contrary to God's Word.

I believe Christians need to stand solidly upon the Rock of Ages who knows all and loves all. His Word was written to guide us in His ways. How can we profess to be His children when condoning behavior He condemned and warned us about?

My mantra for years: protect traditional marriage, defend the unborn.

Tammy

I find it so interesting that one of the threats that face a marriage is insecurity. A person's insecurities don't seem quite so insidious as, say, a pornography addiction. When you hold those two things up, it seems much natural to think of going to war against a threatening addiction than it does to go against something like embarrassments and low self-esteem.

Yet in a relationship, it is deadly to allow guilt to linger or grow. A person who feels inferior or insecure has a hard time fully accepting the love offered by their spouse, and in order to give love wholeheartedly, you have to be able to receive it too. A thing like this can demolish the love in a relationship quietly, insidiously, without either person noticing until it's almost too late.

Looking at it that way, it's much easier to see insecurities as enemies in a relationship, to be powerfully opposed...obliterated with love!

Donna

This business of protecting your spouse stands out to me, maybe because, to a single person, it sounds like a fabulous benefit. But wait—I hear the roar of married masses shouting, "Pipe down, sister! You have no idea what it takes to do this marriage thing."

You're right! But, doing this single thing isn't always all it's cracked up to be, either. And when it comes to protection, singles can't win. There's no spouse watching our backs and other people's spouses are watching us like hawks. I felt like a suspect my first few years in my first church. It was not a welcoming experience, but an isolating one. The ice broke over time, but—yikes!—it was a long, hard slog.

OK. That burr is out of my saddle. And I hope the context is helpful to someone. I treasure the sanctity of other people's marriages and I understand their concerns. Holding together a marriage in today's world isn't easy. Therefore, I'm single *and* protective of married folks—sometimes to a fault.

Shae

Donna, you are the friend whom everyone needs to have, without a doubt! As a single-married-single-married, well, you get the drift, I appreciate that someone does have my back, preferably in prayer. I intend to guard this relationship with my life.

The Internet has probably surpassed television now as a destructive "parasite" as the authors term it, to a marriage. It broke my heart to hear recently from a friend who discovered her 50-year-old husband viewing porn and having relationships with young women in chat rooms. He, thankfully, has agreed to personal counseling and she now has to set parameters and take preemptive action.

No Can Do

Angela

◇◇◇◇◇◇◇◇◇◇◇

Oh, I just *love* my beautiful new shoes!

Daddy used to tell me that "people use the word love too often. The word should be reserved for people—not things." He was right.

Most people *lust* today rather than *love*. I must admit that when I read that Cole Haan was celebrating their 80th anniversary by "re-imagining their classic oh-so-soft-leather penny loafer," I was in lust. It took awhile to save for a pair, but oo-la-la, they are sitting in my closet as I type.

According to the book, lust means "to set your heart and passions on something forbidden." I can't say that I've lusted after much in life—a pair of shoes now and then, and a Jaguar (until they were bought by Ford which completely destroyed the "aura"). Otherwise, we've daily worked hard to gradually improve the quality of our lifestyle—of love, not lust.

Shae

Now you're speaking my language, Angela. Shoes. You know Prada?

I recall those penny loafers; the shiny pennies enamored me more than the shoes did. My oldest sister had a pair but I was still in red patent leather. Mysteriously, her pennies kept disappearing. (Shield your eyes if my halo is too bright.) What can I say? We were poor, and those coins would sound so good going into the little church-shaped offering box that chimed with every deposit.

How easy it was to rationalize then and it is just as easy now. Only when I surrender something to God do I stop reasoning and rationalizing it to the point of making it laudable or justifiable! Sigh. The issue is never the thing I have surrendered—it is surrender itself, and it is another thing when He takes it! Whoa! When I stop vacillating between sunshine and shadow and live out my surrender in all things—ungodly attitudes, lusts of the flesh, unhealthy addictions (white powdered donuts, Prada, pennies)—love by way of sacrificial death rushes in to free me. His life emerges in me as these things die to my control, to my lordship, to running and ruining my life. Perhaps, Angela, soon I will be rummaging in your closet for practical shoes.

Donna

Lust is a blade that cuts all ways. There have been times when a friend's lust for something forbidden has impacted our friendship, even though the issue was not between us. When you get together under those circumstances, it's a creepy threesome: you, your friend, and your friend's secret. Suddenly, you're walking on eggshells; and the more you accommodate the unspoken, the more it steals from the relationship.

I can remember holding my tongue. That is, until that gut-level tipping point appeared and I knew that continuing to ignore the elephant in the room would be, metaphorically speaking, akin to escorting my friend over the nearest cliff.

No can do—even if the alternative proves costly, which it did. One such relationship is now stronger than ever (after a painful season of awkwardness). More importantly, that friend has experienced restoration in her own life. The other relationship never quite recovered. Either way, the risks were worthwhile.

If the high heel were on the other foot, I pray someone would call me on it.

Tammy

I gotta say, looking at lust as a desire for satisfaction in anything but God (rather than the naughty little sexual sin most people would probably associate with the word) makes me realize that this issue is basically an international pandemic of this generation. Even the least materialistic person doesn't escape it. I should know. I've never been too into possessions in general, but I am so far away from lust-free.

There is another side to this, too—another strain of the pandemic virus. When I was discussing this chapter with my super-genius mom, she pointed out that in our culture today, so many people lust after fantasies—particularly fantasies about marriage. She pointed out how we are fed on fairy tales from childhood onward, leading women in particular to dream of marriage as their "happily-ever-after" with Prince Charming. (And young couples can certainly seem like princes and princesses to each other.) When, however, it doesn't turn out to be this way in reality, that lust for the fantasy gets going, sowing dissatisfaction.

The truth our culture needs to know is simple: God is better than romantic fairy tales and possessions. Period.

THE TRAIN WRECK

Shae

Forgiving others has maintained a steady stream of God's blessings flowing in my life, but I have discovered something even better. Forgiveness can lead to the ultimate love connection.

One day, God said, "Shae, I want you to ask "Mary" for forgiveness.

"But Lord," I cried, "I'm not at fault; she should be asking *me* to forgive *her*. She calls me names, she degrades and insults me, shuns me openly, tells the world I'm a horrible person, blames me, when I'm the one who suffered, *yada yada, sniff, whine.*"

"Do it and I promise you a miracle."

At my son's baseball game I caught her eye in the stands and smiled. Lo, a few moments later, she headed toward me. "Mary, I've really missed you." Not sure what I was even asking forgiveness for, and half-heartedly in obedience to God, I pleaded, "Please forgive me."

She went on and on about the perceived misconducts, and finally, "Yes, I forgive you." Well, that went well. Eye-roll please. I half expected her to beg me for forgiveness.

A few months later, Mary's son called. She was in hospice, in the last stage of cancer. "Mom asked for you—she wants you to come and spend a night with her."

An hour later, I was by her side. "Do you want to know Jesus, Mary?" I whispered around midnight.

Through shallow breath, "Yes...yes."

Mary flew into Love's arms the next day. And I have forgiven everyone who has hurt me in my path, since.

Angela

BTW have any of you read *The Shack* by William P. Young? One particular scene left a permanent mark in my spirit. In case you haven't read it I won't give away anything, but the essence is: if you fail to forgive someone, you are actually judging and blaming God for creating that person. Of course the scene in the book is much more vivid and stirring, but this truth continually burns inside.

Who am I not to forgive whatever trivialness I may find horrifying at the time? Who am I not to forgive another human being who was made by the same Creator? Who am I not to forgive someone God loves as much as He loves me?

Who am I? I am forgiven.

Donna

Oh, Angela—*The Shack* is provoking the stuffing out of me right now!

Forgiveness. How can I accept it and then withhold it from others? I can use the "What I Did Isn't As Bad As What They Did" defense. But what happens when I'm on the wrong end of the rationale? Ewww...don't want to go there.

I remember sincerely forgiving a beloved family member who'd hurt me. Then, ten years after she died, I was grilling portobellos in the backyard and thinking about the price of tomatoes, when *bam!* A bolt came out of the blue with this thought: "Remember So-and-so? You haven't *fully* forgiven her."

"No way!" I railed, as my stuffing fell around me.

I basted the mushrooms and saw the problem: I'd never acknowledged the severity of the offense. Doing so would have forced me to admit that someone wonderful was capable of doing something awful. Instead looking the mess in the eye, I simply excused the act.

But Jesus didn't excuse our sin; He bore it. We're forgiven—fully.

Tammy

◇◇◇◇◇◇◇◇◇◇◇

I hadn't thought about it that way, Donna, but your right—it's not really forgiveness if we don't fully recognize the wrong that's been done. It's an excuse, and sometimes it is so much easier to excuse than to forgive.

However, unforgiveness can completely derail a person. I've had at least one train wreck myself as a result, and I've yet to experience a great deal in life. It wasn't even a case of refusing to forgive that caused it—the train wreck happened because I tried to forgive in my own strength. I learned one thing through that, though. We can only truly forgive through the grace of God, who forgave us first.

WHO, ME?

Angela

Taking responsibility for my actions is hard sometimes. It's easier to take the low "it wasn't me" road rather than the high road and fess up. Now that the kids are out of the house, we don't even have them to blame. Now Maggie is the one who leaves the pantry door open and forgets to take the garbage out on Monday nights. Now it's Maggie who didn't mail the insurance payment on time and didn't pick up the dry cleaning. Now it's Maggie who didn't write toilet paper on the grocery list.

But Maggie takes the blame in stride, and as long as her food and water dish are always full, she keeps a wag in her little stubby tail.

Donna

◇◇◇◇◇◇◇◇◇◇◇

Can I borrow Maggie? I could use a scapegoat every now and then. When you're single, the buck stops at the same place all the time. I'm the one who, at one time or another, dropped the roast that slid across the kitchen floor, drove a mile with the emergency brake engaged, launched the toilet paper holder into the you-know-what, and sent the insurance check to the electric company. I have a flat spot from all the slaps I've given myself upside the head for antics like that.

I can only imagine if a mate were handy how apt my pointed finger would be to take aim at him. Like a compass needle drawn to magnetic north, no doubt. And if he were to leave the cap off the toothpaste 730 times a year? Oy!

Hopefully, I would be more responsible to love and cherish him than I give myself credit for. Even so, I'd likely find myself on a fairly steady diet of humble pie.

Shae

◇◇◇◇◇◇◇◇◇◇◇

So, your future mate will brush his teeth twice a day. That's great, go for hygiene...lol. Better that than leaving the toothpaste cap off only 52 times per year. Can you say, "Green and mossy?" How about "snaggletooth?" Ewww.

I am so glad we will live forever in eternity (is that redundant?) —I'll need 5 billion years to do all of the housework I have piled up. Just how far I am behind on household chores only dawned on me when I saw "wash me" written in my son's handwriting in the dust on the coffee table this morning. It's not that I am disorganized or a bad housekeeper, mind you, I've just had a lot of deadlines. Plus, my dog is in heat, and you know how that goes, and I just got back from a trip and it's hard to readjust. And I'm tired, my son has asked me for way too much help on his homework. The power went out a few days this month—on Tuesday vacuuming days, no less, so I had to nix that, and I still can't get the boxes of Christmas decorations to storage because I can't find the key. Oh, and I'm sorry for being so late in responding to your blogs girl-friends, this subject of taking personal responsibility has me completely baffled! Echo. Oy!

Tammy

I really like the question at the end of today's dare. Taking responsibility for failures and shortcomings is more than just a verbal confession. It involves behavior—changing patterns and habits to show the other person that you fully realize your mistakes and are working to correct them. I don't have to be married to attest to the truth of this. I'm a person who lives with people; that's enough.

I'm also a person who promised to stop leaving her dishes in the sink. Oops.

THE SPECK INSPECTOR

Angela

There is a fine line between encouraging your mate to achieve his full potential and discouraging him to seek more. This is when the admonition to find intimacy with your spouse applies. If you don't know your mate's inner yearnings, dreams, aspirations, and motivations, you can't be an effective encourager.

When hubby first retired from the U.S. Army, he floundered for a while career-wise. Finally he applied for a federal government position and voila, he was back in a familiar satisfying groove. My encouragement along the way helped, and at times hindered, the process. But based on the intimate findings I had placed in the recesses of my heart and mind, I knew he wouldn't be happy as an insurance agent, a security manager, or a farm hand. So by encouraging (um, he might call it nagging) him to keep looking, he landed a professionally rewarding position.

Most fortunately, he did the same for me several times throughout the years.

Donna

Foibles are plenty in the life of this flawed individual. You ladies have become privy to some; I've even shared the ones that *might* come to pass given this or that circumstance.

I don't think I have a particularly gilded self-image. I'm well aware of my warts (except for the ones that are hiding in my blind spots) and I'm okay with 'fessing up to my shortcomings (most of the time).

Lest you think I'm habitually self-critical, let me say that encouragement is something I'm good at. Hallelujah! I love to encourage people. I don't stroke them or blow pretty, colored smoke at them. I honestly seek to hearten them. Maybe it's the teacher in me. Whatever it is, it blesses me to give encouragement to others.

That said, if the man who leaves the cap off the toothpaste 730 times a year were to become my husband, would Donna the Encourager yield center stage to Donna the "Speck Inspector"?

God, in Your mercy, please help me to get it right.

Shae

Well Donna, *if* that man were the green mossy snaggletooth type, I think DTE would want to remain on stage for the sake of the family photo archives...lol.

I do have high expectations of my buck—in the areas of love only. Love God. Love me. Love our children. Love my dog. Love my Wally bird. Love my body. Love my cooking. Love my snoring. Love my shopping habits. Everything else I can sweep under the carpet, when I have time for housecleaning...lol. Whatever I can do to encourage Doug's love, I plan on doing—and I suspect that entails loving him hard, and championing his efforts. Tada. Oh my, bless me Father! I was short-winded!

Tammy

I certainly am grateful for folks like you Donna—those with the gift of encouragement. It's so important, for those of us without a lifelong cheerleader to find other relationships with people who are willing to build us up and encourage us. Even more importantly, we *need* mentors and friends who will help us with our weaknesses by calling us on them, and then cheering for us as we work to overcome them. Encouragement is vital...and not just for married folks.

THE PITY PARTY'S OVER

Shae

My age is about to fall off the calendar and I am still on a journey of growth especially relating to personal relationships. But hey, I am not 50, I am 21 with 29 years of experience. Thankfully, I've grown up and don't throw or attend pity parties anymore. This chapter on selflessly meeting the needs of our spouse expounds on sacrificial love beautifully.

I always thought the worst, that somehow whatever my husband was going through was my fault. I gave myself too much credit in my own youthful narcissistic way. It wasn't about me at all, but about him, and very real needs. Somehow, I would get the focus back on me. Hello. God uncovered my faux pas lickety-split. Then of course, I took sacrifice to other extremes, Mother Teresa to the power of ten million or the media's stereotypical portrayal of the guilt-trip laden Jewish mother portrayed ala "How many Jewish mothers does it take to change a light bulb? Answer: (Mournfully, in Yiddish accent), "Don't worry about me; I'll just sit here in the dark." Only when I surrendered my sulking to God could I see my husband's deeper needs. I just wish I'd met more of them.

Angela

◇◇◇◇◇◇◇◇◇◇◇

When the children were young and there were 34 hours worth of work, errands, and taxiing to do in 24, feeling unappreciated was a way of life—for me and hubby. There just didn't seem to be enough time to exchange pleasantries let alone compliments.

I threw my share of self-pity parties over the years. When I wasn't thinking of or doing for our daughters, I was thinking of me-me-me. When our youngest flew away to begin her 5-year, 5-colleges career, hubby and I looked at each other and reintroduced ourselves. Thankfully we rediscovered all the things we enjoyed about each other way back when. The sacrifices we made during the kid chaos years were worth it.

I trust, hope, and pray that my heavenly Father feels the same way about His sacrifice for me.

Donna

◇◇◇◇◇◇◇◇◇◇◇◇

Ever been caught in one of those "Betcha Can't Top My Bad News" conversations? A family wedding. The arugula salad is served. Second Cousin Woe-Is-Me launches a commiseration campaign about how difficult 13-year-olds can be and how awful it is that the family is cursed with some genetic predisposition or other.

Ugh—pass the Pepto. Avoiding gossip and the negativity that travels with it is a pastime of mine (maybe more of an extreme sport, considering what it takes to ski around those moguls).

If only it burned calories! Alas, serve me a beefy conversation any day, one I can sink my heart into—an *authentic* exchange that, by definition, fuels the metabolism of life. "Yes, Waiter, I'll have the High-Protein Relationship-Nourishing Communication Platter, please. Yes, I realize it's also high-fiber and could raise some temporary…uh…issues."

Which is not to say that I've never partaken of an empty-calorie conversation. Above all, what I really need to cultivate is the nourishing love that will *listen* to the distress signals Second Cousin Woe-Is-Me is sending and "respond to the heart of the problem."

Tammy
◇◇◇◇◇◇◇◇◇◇◇

This may sound a little strange, but I really almost envy some of you married folks on this one, simply because it seems to me that you often have the power and are in the position to sacrifice and meet your spouse's needs.

Now, maybe I'd feel a little less eager to sacrifice if I were married for a while. That could well be. But from where I am now, one of the most frustrating struggles I face on a regular basis is being powerless to help the needs that I see. Financial, emotional, they seem to be simply everywhere, and I can pray and pray (and I certainly do) but I'm at a loss! There never seems to be anything I can do for the person. I hate feeling like I'm stuck being the useless person in James 2:16: "If one of you says to him, 'Go, I wish you well; keep warm and well fed,' but does nothing about his physical needs, what good is it?"

I guess I just want to encourage you married people to enjoy the privilege of your position. You have the power to meet another person's needs, maybe even to give them a bit of happiness. That's a blessing.

BINGO!

Angela

What motivates most people? Money, recognition, and power come to mind when I think in worldly terms. Love, mercy, and faith in God come to mind when thinking in Christian terms. Stark differences between the two groups of words.

When choosing a career after my late-in-life college education, I opted for a position with a Christian nonprofit organization that establishes hospitals in third-world countries for disabled children. The motivation was apparent. After a few years of daily driving too many miles on an ever-increasing-death toll interstate, I chose to accept a position with a Christian book publisher. Again, the motivation is apparent.

Whether in careers, marriages, or relationships, love should be the motivating factor—after that everything else falls into place very nicely.

Tammy

◇◇◇◇◇◇◇◇◇◇◇

Ooh, motivation. Here's a conscience-pricker. Out of all the things we do every day, little and big, good and bad, almost a hundred percent of the time our reasons for acting the way we do are between us and God. More times than not, I'd have to admit I'm happy to keep it that way.

It's up to you and I to be honest with ourselves about our motivations. We have to be willing to confront ourselves on this issue, with a lot of heavenly help. Sometimes, after all, we need God to show us what our true motivation really is— it can be that hard to figure out. It's tricky...and often, very convicting.

Especially for me.

Donna

◇◇◇◇◇◇◇◇◇◇◇

Funny you should mention motivations, Tammy. Just today, as I prayed for wisdom regarding a particular concern, I was reminded about what seemed to be a totally unrelated issue from 30 years ago. I scratched my head and wondered, *What's this about?*

Completely at a loss to understand, I tried to do what is for me the hardest thing of all: be still and listen. No asking questions, no flipping through the concordance, no nothing but waiting. After what was roughly an eternity, it hit me:

although the situations were dissimilar, something about the way I handled the earlier situation was instructive in the present tense.

It was a matter of motivations. Thirty years ago, I lived on my own steam and made some decisions based on the instinct of self-protection. These choices did not reflect God's will or consider the grace He offered. Nor did they take into account how I might better serve others.

Today's reminder was a gut check to make sure I was on the right track. Thank You, Lord. Message received.

Shae

Bingo. To depend on finite human love alone to motivate one's love is asking for disappointment. Only infinite love will never fail us, and what a beautiful thought, to honor God, who is Love Himself, with our mutual devotion and sincerity. What a burden lifter for a couple to know that Love Divine supplies their needs—the pressure isn't on either imperfect person to deliver. It is so much better than loving through the back door.

THE SAME BUT DIFFERENT

Angela

In the Western world of "me first" and the importance placed on our "individuality," the concept of unity is many times used only during school pep rallies, or when some political party is trying to convince someone of something.

Unity to me doesn't mean that we have to think, say, act, react, or even believe the same thing. Unity within marriages or any relationship means choosing to be together in spite of and because of our differences. In unity we—couples, friends, family, neighbors, coworkers, peers—complement each other. If God wanted us to be the same, He could have created Adam and Eve and then cloned them over and over.

Instead, he created us in unity as individuals. How we respond to others' differences tests our commitment to Him and His creation.

Shae

Speaking of cloning, I have a twin brother and it always makes me laugh when people ask, "Are you identical?" I am um...a slim build...so it is not a surprising question, but I am like, "duh," nevertheless! While we certainly do share similar characteristics and some features, thankfully, Alex and I are quite different. He's balding while I'm getting hairier...lol. Praise the Lord, my parents did not dress us the same.

We were close though and that was bonus. God knew what He was doing; we needed each other, Alex and I, especially when we bounced around from children's homes to foster homes as youngsters and teens. He took it upon himself to be my protector and sported many black eyes because of it. What a support he was to me. I in turn nurtured him as best as I could; he was scared of the dark and of being alone. We still love each other dearly today.

I guess in this respect, Angela, God created my twin brother and I in unity, as you say, as individuals. Not at all unlike a marriage relationship except that I am really glad I didn't marry him!

Tammy

Once again, I'm just a tad in the dark. ^_^ I have no idea what this feels like and no experiences of anything close to this to share. I just think it's amazing that God has given husbands and wives a chance to be a picture of His nature (the unity of the Trinity), plus an earthy image of Christ and the Church. Two for one!

I pray your marriage will be uniquely beautiful, so that when people look at you, they get a hankering to know your loving, relational God.

Donna

◇◇◇◇◇◇◇◇◇◇◇

Like Tammy, I haven't experienced unity in marriage; but I know unity when I see it.

Having been in bands and worked long-term for several organizations, I've witnessed the ebb and flow of organizational life, including long, harmonious periods during which everyone was "on the same team." No matter how long the days or how challenging the task, laughter and good cheer were abundant. Amazing things were accomplished, relationships grew sweeter over time, and everyone enjoyed personal and professional growth.

But, every once in awhile, unity would be tested, whether by an attitude or an action. Most often, with careful attention, the breach was resealed; but if the issue was not addressed, the buoyant atmosphere would turn thick. Distrust would become the coin of the realm and cliques would form. Sadly—very sadly, everything else would begin to decline. It's the *"confusion and every evil work"* syndrome described in James 3:16.

My heart breaks for those who experience disunity in marriage; and my prayers go with them.

PART IV

Love and Eternity

ARE YOU STILL HERE?

Angela

My parents raised my sister, brother, and me to be independent thinkers and self-sufficient individuals. This framework served me well, especially since Mom passed away when I was 23—and 10 days before my wedding 31 years ago. Instilling confidence and self-reliance in children gives them the ability to look beyond the "nest" to worldwide possibilities. Can young adults really find fulfillment when they think of themselves only as their parent's child rather than their own stand-alone person?

Leaving a comfortable place is always scary. When we stored all our household goods, packed our bags and moved to Hawaii for three years, I was as scared as I was excited. When our youngest opted to study in Italy—she was thrilled and apprehensive. When our eldest moved her family to Florida to escape the dreary Pennsylvania winters, it was a challenge that turned out to be a wonderful decision for her.

A dare that I challenge myself with from time to time: leave behind whatever is holding me back from all that God has for me.

Tammy

◇◇◇◇◇◇◇◇◇◇◇

This chapter isn't joking when it talks about how hard separating oneself from one's parents and committing to another person can be. Of course, I haven't left home to get married, but I've heard from my parents how rocky it can be...and I've seen the long-lasting results.

My mom and dad got married 10 days before Christmas. My dad's family—all Catholic—had not seen him for Christmas in two years because he'd been out of the country, and apparently they expected to see him this year at last. However, my mom wanted to be with her family, for many good reasons of her own. My dad played the dutiful new husband, going with what was best for her and taking that job seriously.

Suffice to say, the family wasn't happy. Things have mellowed since then—it's not like we're estranged from that half of the family in some kind of feud—but the point is, even the best families sometimes aren't ready for a son or daughter to take off on their own. That, however, doesn't excuse the married couple from following God's direction to be united to one another. It's tough, but it's gotta be done for the sake of unity.

My parents (jokingly, I hope) add to this that if I never marry, they never have to let me go. ^_^

Donna

My parents didn't raise my brother and me to be clinging vines. Take my first day of kindergarten: it must have been a pretty big a deal for Mom (especially since I was her first-born), but if she had any apprehensions about letting her "baby" go, she never let on. She dressed me in a brand-new outfit, handed me my Roy Rogers pencil case and walked me to P.S. 153, my freshly-cut bangs rustling in the fall breeze.

Mom placed me in the able care of Mrs. Forno, kissed me goodbye, and went home. Chances are she shed a tear along the way. I'll never know.

When Mom picked me up at noon and asked how the day went, I answered with a question: "Mom, why were all those kids crying?" I had no clue what all the fuss was about. Mom did, of course. I'm sure she was relieved to learn that I wasn't among the melted-down ones.

There's another sure thing: she prepared me well for my first and subsequent "leaving" experiences. Thanks Mom!

Shae

◇◇◇◇◇◇◇◇◇◇◇

At our birth, we are in our weakest and most hazardous time of existence. As soon as we leave that intimate place, we cry for someone to hold us, to be near, to be close, and to connect. The loveable Gracie Allen said, "When I was born I was so surprised I didn't talk for a year and a half!" Birth is a shocker—as is leaving the warmth of home, leaving tried and trusted connections for new relationships.

As a foster child, I was no stranger to parting ways and adjusting to new digs and new people. I had no choice. Sure it was difficult and sometimes shocking to be pulled from a place that I had grown used to, but how blessed I was in retrospect to know the love of many mothers and fathers and have their collective wisdom in my life. The downside was the cleaving part. Could I find someone to love who would keep me forever? Not in my first marriage, (what a shocker) but I am certain that I have now.

"EWWW!"

Angela

All I have to say is that this area of marriage (S E X) is nothing like you see in the movies, on the daytime soaps, what you heard in high school, or what your mother told you.

I'll save you my details as my mind flashes back to the reaction of Toula in the scene from the movie *My Big Fat Greek Wedding* when her mother, while having her chin hairs plucked, tells her daughter about "the wedding night" and Toula says, "Ewww, please let that be the end of your speech."

Tammy

Without sounding too argumentative here, can I borrow the

soap box for a bit?

Why don't married people want to tell the rest of us what this is really like? Is it the awkward factor? A lingering idea of traditional "decency"? Just an assumption that we'll hear it from our own parents, or find out for ourselves?

You've already said it—what we hear in the media and in the world today are lies. But guess what? If Christian married people don't stand up and start boldly telling the truth about sex, the lies go unchallenged. Young people hear nothing else!

Why should we feel compelled to keep the truth hush-hush? The Bible talks about it! I think there is a great need among young people to hear the truth in a present-day, down-to-earth way, a way that combats and drives back our culture's false teachings about sex. If the Christian voice is silent, treating the topic like some kind of naughty, unspeakable thing, the only voice left speaking is the one that speaks lies—"Sex is fun; sex is casual; it can't hurt you to enjoy yourself, express yourself, just like everyone else."

I'm sorry if it sounds like I'm "calling you out" or anything, Angela—I really don't mean to. I just want to say this to all married couples who know the truth about God's design for sex and aren't telling it. And I'll stop ranting now. ^_^

Shae

The Bible really does contain mature subject matter in the context of marriage. "Holy sex" is hard for many Christians to wrap their heads around. Sadly, the very word has become an archenemy of the church. Philip Yancey in *Rumors of Another World* did an historical study and found that over the centuries, church authorities issued edicts forbidding the act of sex "period" on certain days. Thursdays, the day of Christ's arrest, Fridays, the day of His death, Saturdays in honor of Mary, and so on. By the time that they covered 40-day fasts, holidays, observances, and a woman's "unclean" days, only 44 "legal" days a year to have sex remained. Talk about inhibiting sex! And contrary to Bible teaching. The biblical account of the king and the Shulamite woman proves that physical love in a marital relationship should be exciting, frequent, and uninhibited.

I am all for a Song of Solomon blockbuster "mature subject matter" Christian movie. Perhaps it will dispel the myth that Christian marriage is anything but prudish, uptight, or formal in the bedroom! Speaking of that, I highly recommend married couples role-play the Shulamite and Solomon's bedroom scene. Ooh la-la. Put on nothing but a veil and listen for your lover's return...lol.

Donna

◇◇◇◇◇◇◇◇◇◇◇

Before getting married, just about everybody wants to find a mate...to belong to someone. I remember the high school custom of wearing an ankle bracelet or a boy's class ring. It was what every girl wanted: to have these symbols say *I am So-and-So's girlfriend. I am attached to someone else.*

Fast-forward 10 or 15 years. Some married friends were already fed up with being attached. Instead of getting goose bumps, they developed worry warts and were weary of their husbands' "demands" for sex. Gone was the youthful yearning to *belong* to someone else. Doleful wives would tell me, "Donna, marriage isn't all it's cracked up to be."

The grass is always greener, I guess. And, surely, there are ups and downs to a couple's life, sexually and otherwise. How would I approach my husband's sexual and emotional needs? Would I willingly pay the price to win his heart?

That sounds hard to do. Then again, being single isn't a day at the beach, either.

33

DIVVY UP THE LOAD

Angela

When hubby would have to travel because of his job, for the first few days it was great. I could fix a bowl of cereal for dinner at 4 o'clock. I could take an hour-long bubble bath whenever the mood struck. I could eat cookies and watch an all-day Monk marathon. I could spend a whole entire day shopping! (Although I could do all these things even if he wasn't away on business, it just seemed like I was a bit more free (as in self-guilt free) to do them when he was gone.)

But after a few days, I always felt like part of me was missing. He is the sympathetic ear that listens when I'm whining about the neighbor, a coworker, taxes. He is Mr. Pro/Con when I'm stuck with a hard decision. He is my defender when I think someone is being unfair. He is the other usually "better" half of me who keeps me sane. I'd like to think he'd say the same of me.

Shae

Well Angela, two better halves must make a better whole, right? As I see it, in marriage, it is not that two halves have come together to become a whole—two whole people join to become one body, uniting in love. So if two people in marriage become a whole, that is, one completes the other, wouldn't it make sense that if a couple splits, there is not one split but two? The man separates from part of himself and the woman separates from part of herself.

Ouch. And greater ouch in light of how it affects the equation of "we multiply one another's joys and divide one another's sorrow." Suddenly, joy divides and sorrow multiplies. We become Adam or Eve in the garden alone. I chime in with what God said in the beginning in reference to Adam's aloneness. Not good.

Donna

The idea that "love completes each other" is so big, so amazing, so God, that I want to shout, "Being married *is* all it's cracked up to be!"

The complementary relationship cannot be beat. How wonderful to convert your differences into advantages. How smart to divvy up the load of whatever it is that must be understood, accomplished, overcome, or carried each and every day (Being chief cook *and* bottle-washer all the time can wear you out!).

When my car acts up, I'd love to say, "Honey, the car is making that noise again." Even if my husband were clueless about cars, sharing the issue with him would be reassuring. How cool would it be for him to stand across the counter from the mechanic instead of me? Let's see Mr. Auto Fixer Guy try to snow Mr. Husband Man with talk of non-existent foo-foo valves and yada-yada belts.

Obviously, love completes us in much bigger ways than that. All of it sounds very good to me. :-)

Tammy

◇◇◇◇◇◇◇◇◇◇◇

Obviously, completing one another is a big and very significant thing. But here's a small and seemingly insignificant story about it.

My mom had to make our family's beloved Taco Salad Spread platter for the Superbowl. (We just couldn't watch the Steelers beat the Cardinals without it!) It's delicious and she does a great job, but she always gets frustrated when she tries to spread the (firmer) cheese layer over the (softer) bean layer. She can never get it to spread nicely.

This time, however, Dad was on hand with his "fix the

problem" brain. And Dad came up with the clever idea to spread the cheese layer out on wax paper, then transfer it onto the bean dip. Mom picked up on the brilliant notion, they executed it together, and voila! The best, most beautiful Taco Salad Spread ever made. Complementary skills and teamwork save the day!

And they had a blast doing it. ^_^

ONE AT A TIME

Shae

Hello? Tammy, you have the nerve to sign off without giving us the recipe for that yummy Taco Salad Spread? Waiting.

I live to glorify God, and to that end, I try to be godly in everything I do, but I have failed miserably. My marriage failed in that respect. I think the apostle Paul nailed it when he encouraged his young protégé Timothy to *train* himself in godliness. He didn't tell him to *try* to be godly. The prize at the end of the race in marriage most precious to me would be someone pointing at us and saying, "I didn't know marriage could look like that!"

Angela

I know for a fact that if we didn't have God as our foundation, our marriage would be in shambles. Realizing that God is the solid Rock upon which a marriage can endure is the only way to stand strong against the daily barrage of worldly, fleshly, self-centered, hate, compromise, abuse, and absolute lack of moral virtue that is tossed at us from the television, radio, newspapers, and Internet.

It is painful when I think about why some of other faiths look at the United States of America and call us evil. Who can blame them? Flipping through almost any magazine or clicking by almost any commercial would surely cause many of our grandmothers to blush, and now those with strong convictions to rail. (Remember that reaction—to blush—do people even do that anymore?)

What happened to our nation? How can we become a country that exemplifies godly values and morals? One person at a time—one marriage at a time.

Donna

◇◇◇◇◇◇◇◇◇◇◇

One person at a time. It is disheartening to see our young people steeped in a nihilistic culture where regard for others—and for *self*—is diminishing by the day. I guess that's all the more reason to celebrate and encourage goodness by "catching" others in godly acts.

Thanks to online networking, I've been able to reconnect with former students I wouldn't otherwise be able to locate.

Most of them are in their 20s and early 30s. (Where did the time go?) They have careers, families, and the headaches that go with adulthood. But they have something else, the thought of which flows over my heart like warm honey. It's the evidence of godliness in their lives. They're holding fast to what their parents, pastors, and teachers taught them. They're not perfect people, but they've made biblical values their own and, now, their children are following in their footsteps.

How perfectly wonderful!

Tammy

OK, OK, recipe coming soon Shae! Lol.

I think both of you have definitely pointed out something cool about godliness: we grow in the Lord individually, yes, but that doesn't mean we should ever disregard the fabulous relational aspect of godliness. Whether in a marriage or with trusted Christian peers, one of the best things about growing closer to the Lord is the encouragement of others. You get to encourage them in their walk, see their growth, and be encouraged by it, as well as receive the direct encouragement others give.

God is relational, and we get to become more like Him in an amazing way through deep, connected relationships.

SNOWFLAKES AND FINGERPRINTS

Angela

Finding a helpful marriage mentor may be harder than the book explains. After all, marriages, even long-lasting ones, are just two imperfect people paddling hard upstream to keep from capsizing. What works for one couple may be completely wrong for another. Case in point: I have several friends who serve a full course dinner every night because their husbands "expect" it—even now that the children have flown the coop. This would not work at our house. Other friends couldn't even imagine us moving to Hawaii "and leaving your friends and family behind!?" These married couples have been happy for decades—because they are comfortable within their own special relationships.

I think I'd have to add a caution to today's dare. Marriages are as unique as snowflakes—don't try and stuff yours into someone else's concept of what works.

Tammy

Angela, I think that's definitely true, and not just of older married couples that offer guidance to younger ones. In any relationship like this, both need to be careful—it's so easy, when you're looking to someone for advice and coaching in life, to forget that what works for them may not be something you should reproduce exactly in your own life.

Even outside of marriage, I can say for sure that it's not easy to build a good relationship based on seeking guidance as one grows—a relationship that guides the younger person into success in God's unique path for them. In spite of the difficulty, however, I truly believe it is priceless to receive council from the older generation. It is certainly worth pursuing... and I say that as a reminder to myself, as well. To-do list: keep ears open for good advice!

Donna

Accountability is a God thing, but I agree with Angela: it's not a one-size-fits-all proposition. When choosing to whom you'll be accountable, choose carefully. That said, there's a lot of untapped freedom to be released through mentoring relationships.

My parents were children of The Great Depression. They

were amazing, upright people. I'm proud of their integrity and all they taught my brother and me. They worked hard and took care of their own, including their own families and their own issues. They plowed through the ups and downs of marriage and sorted out their concerns alone. Perhaps they believed that marital imperfections spoke ill of them as people; I really don't know. (Don't most of us get caught up in the performance-versus-authentic-identity trap somewhere along the line?)

In any case, I truly believe that when we open our hearts to trusted friends, we learn that our "misses," marital or otherwise, aren't so unusual. What a guilt-and-shame-buster that is...and how freeing to any relationship!

Note to self.

Shae

Some couples take things a little too far in involving third parties in their relationship and I would put a caveat in to remember that marriage is about leaving and cleaving! Another caveat, do not use a third party to back only you up. Ditto, do not trash your partner in front of that third party. Hey, I'm a preacher, imagine that!

Running home to mama or our friends every time something goes wrong does not strengthen or mature a relationship at all. There are times to involve wise others in the absence of common ground but some people tell everyone their business.

The Shulamite woman was so upset when she realized that she had missed Solomon she ran everywhere looking for him. When she could not find him, the distressed woman appealed to her girlfriends (lots of paraphrasing here), "Hey, if you see Solomon, tell him I miss him so."

Their response was, "What is so special about this guy that he drives you to this? You're so beautiful—the world is your oyster, men would marry you on a dime, you could have anyone you want!" (see Song of Solomon 5:8-9).

I am sure they meant well but their remarks could have planted bad seed in their exquisite garden of love.

GOD'S LOVE LETTER

Donna

◇◇◇◇◇◇◇◇◇◇

"Be in it...stay under it...live it." That's excellent advice about God's Word, but as I read "Day 36" I felt the urge to add a thought of my own.

You might chalk up that urge to a bad case of Writers' OCD. However, you'd be wrong. OK, you'd be partly right. So here's my thought: Sticking with God's Word isn't as much about our effort to commit as it is about the transforming power of His love. "Love is God's Word." It melts the hardest of human hearts. (It cracked this tough nut!)

That love draws me up into the Father's lap. Once there, I drop the facades and soak in the warm bath of His Word. I don't squawk—even when He washes behind my ears!

Receiving His love empowers me to love Him back and to

stick with His Word.

Tammy

Donna, I certainly agree. I've found in my own life that when I'm soaking in the reality of God's love, reading His Word becomes my favorite part of the day. Because it's true—it's His love, and it just takes over. Getting up early isn't a chore—God's Word made an early-riser out of this night person! Spending a certain amount of time reading and praying isn't hard at all—rather than checking the clock every few minutes, I'd have to set an alarm to remind myself when I needed to stop! Nothing else can do this but His love; it transforms us, it makes Him so addicting, and then it just permeates the rest of the day.

And I can only tell you about how it rocked a single girl's world. I can only imagine how He can rock a marriage with His love!

Angela

During one of our detours from mainstream denomination church land, we attended a small local church and I attended a small group Bible study once a week. A few years after this group disbanded, I attended a Bible study led by a kind and gentle neighbor. I also was involved in noontime Bible fellowships when I worked for the government and for a small liberal arts college. I learned a lot about God's Word through these discussions with other believers.

Although our mainstream church also offered Bible studies, I didn't feel as free to offer my opinion or perspective. I didn't have the "expected" answers.

Today I enjoy my private discussions with God about His Word. Every time I open my well-worn King James Version, the more insight I gain into our heavenly Father. The answers to all of life's questions are found in the Bible.

Shae

Only the names have been changed, Angela. We can see ourselves within the Good Book's pages. The Bible actually tells the story of my life and condition. I fit right in with the wandering and waffling children of Israel, with Job and his suffering, (though I have a donut pad for my boils), and had I been the first woman in the world I don't know that I wouldn't have eaten of the forbidden fruit. Most of all, the Bible is God's mind in print, and we glimpse it! The Bible is, was, and always will be my love manual, and is the one book I keep copies of all over the house. Yes girls, even in *that room!* @@

"Now I Lay Me…"

Donna

◇◇◇◇◇◇◇◇◇◇

To see agreement in prayer as a kind of "harmonic symphony" makes sense to me. Jesus said in Matthew 18:19-20: *"If two of you agree here on earth concerning anything you ask, My Father in heaven will do it for you. For where two or three gather together as My followers, I am there among them"* (NLT).

The effect of two people aligning themselves (in real time) with God Himself has "good" written all over it. I can almost hear the perfect resonance of a cosmic pitchfork as that prayer gets underway!

It's no substitute for one-on-one time with God, the kind of personal prayer Angela talked about. Three *can* be a crowd. But as an added dimension of prayer, this sounds to this single dame like an attractive marital perk.

Angela

◇◇◇◇◇◇◇◇◇◇◇◇

Hubby and I do not routinely pray together. Maybe we should, but we don't. Praying together makes you vulnerable and reveals deep thoughts, dreams, concerns, and disappointments. Our relationship with God is very personal, and I don't think either of us wants to share that secret, intimate relationship with anyone but Him—even through prayer together.

I agree with everything *The Love Dare* has to say about praying together, and there is no doubt that bonding in this way is very special. But when I climb up into Father God's lap to have a heart-to-heart, I prefer that conversation to be one on One. I am His child first.

In our own way we pray together, and have for many years. Although our prayers may not be aloud while holding hands, our one voice has reached Him—of this I have no doubt.

Tammy

◇◇◇◇◇◇◇◇◇◇◇◇

Boy, my question on this chapter was going to be, "How do you *do* this?" However, it looks like I'm not the only one who finds this dare a little challenging. To me, so long accustomed to a completely solo walk, just God and me, just the *idea* of sharing prayer with someone else on a regular basis feels like something well outside my comfort zone. I appreciate Angela's reminder that it *is* OK to keep some of the relationship with the Lord personal. I really like mine that way. ^_^

At the same time, I can't deny that the benefits of getting outside of your comfort zone, of vulnerability, are immense. I hope that in the coming decades of singleness, I won't forget how to open up to other people that way.

Shae

It takes some getting used to, I'll give it that, but the benefits are enormous. Prayer has created such depth of companionship, intimacy, and love in my relationship with Doug. How thrilling to pray with him and lay bare our souls before the Lord. It has added a beautiful and vital element to our faith, intimacy, and oneness, and is like the icing on the cake after my personal time with the Lord. Bliss! Of course, prayer is not only in speaking to the Lord, but in listening for His voice and hearing Him answer us. Whoa—it rocks when we "hear" Him together. We are like, "Thank You GOD!"

Yes, we become vulnerable but praying together has built mutual trust, has encouraged humility and honesty, has raised the joy factor, has deepened our communication, and has strengthened our faith in the Lord and in each other. Remember, "Two are better than one because they have a good return for their labor." We labor in prayer for each other, for our families, and our friends, and see "miraculous times two" results!" Of course, the best thing of all, our children see us pray together—that has to do something for their future relationships! I pray so!

REALITY DAY DREAMS

Angela

Do you know what your spouse would really like? Ouch! I know the answer to that question and I know I am holding him back from having his desire.

I push this desire out of my mind almost daily, and instead focus on the other "easy" dreams that cause me less angst. Take him to Ruth's Chris for Valentine's Day dinner this year; make that special dish he likes and exceeds my no-more-than-5-ingredients rule; not interrupt when NASCAR is on—those kind of dreams.

But when it comes to seriously considering selling our high-maintenance home sweet home and moving permanently back to high-rise living in Hawaii, I just can't seem to make that sacrifice. My excuses: grandchildren, friends, fall, winter, spring, and how our best furry friend could not survive the year-round summer heat.

Donna

Angela, that *is* tough. Hmmm...what would I do in your shoes? I do know I'd give up my pad in a heartbeat. Of course, I'm not emotionally invested in my third-floor walk up (although I am keen on Colorado). It would be easy for me to score points with a new husband by saying, "Yes, honey. Of course I'll move to Hawaii with you." What a sacrifice! (LOL) But it would be an empty one.

There have been times when I sensed God nudging me this way or that, yet I dragged my heels. Was I really unsure of His voice or was I hoping He would change His mind? Probably a little of both. Would a prospective husband hold more sway with me than the Creator of the universe? Not likely.

The good news is that I am getting better at saying, "Yes"— promptly and joyfully. Still, I'd surely have to lean on the Father to faithfully meet my hubby's desires in the way He would want me to.

Tammy

My grandpa takes my grandma up to their house in Nova Scotia, Canada, for the entire summer every year, and has done so for over 50 years now. Of course, he enjoys the trip too—summers in Canada are much more manageable than in North Carolina—but for her, it's a dream. So, even when he'd like to head home early, they stay for as long as she wants. He's been making her dream come true for over 50 years; it's truly amazing to me.

Shae

Do you know what gets me? Ridiculously rich kadzillion-aires who live in poverty their whole lives and then leave their fortunes to a duck. What a waste! They never lived the life they could have with their riches. Money oozing everywhere yet never touching it to ease burdens, never even dipping into it to transform a life, feed a hungry mouth, help fulfill someone's dream, never mind their own. Quackers! (groan).

Guilty as charged! In truth, I am no better at times when I pray. Here I have access to my Father's riches, to His vast resources, to the treasures of heaven. I mean, what *doesn't* God have or what can't He supply; and I ask My Father, who happens to be the King of the Universe, the Creator of billions of galaxies, each one containing hundreds of billions of stars, all named mind you, for chopped liver. Hello? If I'm in Him and He is in me I should be oozing the stuff! Of course I'm not just talking money. It's time I acted like a princess with access to her Daddy's wealth, reach into His vastness, dip into the treasure and pull on heaven's extravagance for my family. Yeah. Dream big because my Daddy's big. Maybe there will even be a little roast duck left over for pooch Gracie.

ARE YOU KIDDING ME?

Angela

God's unconditional love is our model. In our sound-byte society, nothing lasts for very long—if it does, we're amazed.

Our son-in-law's aunt and uncle were married for 72 years. Amazing.

Charlton Heston and his wife were married for 65 years. Amazing.

Brittney Spears was married twice: once for two years and another marriage lasted 55 hours. Typical.

Tossing away a marriage is easy. Committing to love the same person for a lifetime can be hard, but not impossible. God is always faithful to give us the answers when we ask Him.

Hubby and I didn't ask Him for answers during our first marriages. As this is the second marriage for both of us, we know

now that only with God's unconditional love as our model can we finish this life until death do us part.

Donna
◇◇◇◇◇◇◇◇◇◇◇

Day 39 cuts to the quick. It makes me wish I were married so I could take the dare. As I say that, my mind is filled with the memories of painful Frasier-Crane-like moments from past relationships: Take the Valentine's Day when I learned that Jon (the thoughtful man I described in Chapter 4) had failed to mention his new and quite serious relationship to me. *Ouch!* And the Valentine's Day when another boyfriend gave me a three-foot-high card and then announced that he was calling it quits. *Are you kidding me?*

Let's get off the subject of Valentine's Day—quick!

I can only imagine the importance of God's grace in helping married people to love their spouses *no matter what.* It is the ultimate love dare and one I can't imagine taking without God's help.

Tammy
◇◇◇◇◇◇◇◇◇◇◇

It's true—our world is filled with failing love. It is everywhere, it is almost expected—certainly, my generation has grown up accustomed to temporary love. We like to keep our expectations low, thinking it will help diffuse some of the pain we feel when love dies.

It doesn't work. Even when we believe from the beginning that love is just as likely to fail as not, a part of the human heart is still longing, always longing for this perfect, unfailing love. We can't turn off this deep need for God's love, which He built into us right from the start.

As a result, no matter how common failed love becomes, and no matter how casual we try to be about it, it still hurts. It still damages people and wounds them deeply, and they are still left longing for real, unfailing love. For Him.

Shae

I saw marriage as a journey to forever. Imagine my disappointment when it died. It took me five years to heal. I have grown closer to God as a result.

For marriage to last it has to go through a constant renewal process just as God continually renews creation to prevent the world from wearing out, which it would do if He doesn't continue His acts of creation every day, and just as He had to renew me.

My ex-husband and I didn't have to live in Never Ever Happy Land, we could have taken many of the biblical precepts presented in this book, to renew and create new beginnings together. But without inviting Love Himself to weave His supernatural grace and mercy through us, forever betrothal was nigh impossible. We needed to imitate God in renewing that which was there at the creation of our marriage, create the things that weren't, and pull on Heaven for that which we couldn't in and of ourselves change, for 'til death do us part" to even have a chance. Hindsight won't change things, but devotion to the Author of Love, will most certainly transform.

THE ULTIMATE VOW-KEEPER

Angela

I've heard of couples renewing their marriage vows but have never seriously considered it. Mostly because I doubt hubby would really be into it. But if I suggested we have the ceremony in Hawaii—who knows?! Aloha!

Donna

Covenant with God is what "keeps" me. I have *the* perfect Partner in this life, the sweet One and Only who loves me more than I'll ever understand, the Saving One who watches my back even as I sleep.

I'll take this final dare by composing a fresh statement of my faith in Him and in the covenant of His love. As I read my "vows" aloud, I will yield to the love that draws me deeper into the velvet folds of that eternal bond.

Whether He entrusts me to a husband and a husband to me, or simply gives me the strength for forever-singleness, I am a "kept" woman...happily and wholeheartedly His.

Tammy

God is the perfect covenant-keeper. His vows to us are eternal, no matter what. And it's His covenant love for us that has the power to sustain us and heal us, even when the strongest human covenants are broken. He's still there. He still loves. And His covenant with us bears all our weaknesses and failings. He's the flawless face of love, and His covenant promise is the single most romantic thing I can think of.

Shae

I hear that Heaven is a place with streets of pure gold that reflect Heaven's glories as a mirror. I am sure the reflection is that "flawless Face of Love." We need the God of Forever and Ever and Ever and Ever in our Until Death Do Us Part relationships because there really can be Heaven on earth with the King of Love reigning in our hearts and lives.

I'm glad for our time reflecting in The Powder Room. In our

covenant to review this book together, I've seen the light of His unconditional love, mercy, and grace in your reflections, even through my "Ouch Chihuahua!" chigger moments.

Well who knew? Our lives can be a fairy tale after all, a Happily Ever After in the love of God Most High, in the love of the God who has relentlessly pursued us, who has remained faithfully with us, married or single and young or not so young, and who has loved us more than we can ever imagine! While our marriages and singleness' are journeys to forever, our relationship with God is already by covenant in forever. With God's love manifesting through each one of us, there will be no weak links in the chains of our relationships and if there are, the God who can transform water into wine, will certainly strengthen, and empower for transformation.

Epilogue

Well, my apprehension about venturing into The Powder Room was unfounded. What I found there was indeed all the "essentials"...and more! There was clean refreshing water flowing from newfound friends, and there was just enough light from The Light to reveal some flaws that we need to work on. Not only was there "a" lady to hand me something soft to dry my face and hands, there were "three" such women who brought tears of joy and sadness to my eyes and reminders that we are His hands here on earth.

The chairs were indeed very comfortable, so much so that we easily exceeded our allotted powder-puff me-time together. The reflections we saw in The Powder Room mirror through *The Love Dare* book brought back fond and haunting memories, current hair-curling circumstances, and hope for shiny bright futures.

Meet us here again when we walk through the woods to *The Shack,* the best-selling book by William P. Young.

BONUS

TAMMY'S MOM'S
TACO SALAD SPREAD RECIPE

1 16-oz. can refried beans

1/2 cup taco sauce

3/4 cup shredded cheddar cheese

1 8-oz. package softened (room temperature) cream cheese

1/4 cup sour cream

3 tablespoons mayonnaise

1/4 tsp. garlic powder

2 cups guacamole (approx)

1 diced tomato

1/2 cup sliced black olives

1/2 cup chopped green onions

Mix together refried beans and taco sauce. (Optional: add a few dashes of hot sauce.) Spread in a thick, even layer over a serving plate.

Thoroughly blend softened cream cheese, mayonnaise, sour cream, and garlic powder until smooth and lumpless. Spread evenly over bean layer. (Extremely clever trick thought up by Tammy's dad: Lay out a sheet of clear plastic wrap, and place the cream cheese mixture in the center. Place another sheet of plastic wrap over that, and roll out cream cheese into desired shape and thickness between the plastic wrap. Then, remove top piece of plastic and transfer entire layer onto the bean layer.)

Spread guacamole evenly over cream cheese layer. (Guacamole can be made any way you like, but Tammy prefers homemade from avocados over store-bought.)

Sprinkle diced tomatoes evenly over guacamole layer. Repeat with sliced olives, chopped green onions, and finally, top with shredded cheddar cheese.

Serve immediately or chill in refrigerator until needed. Serve with tortilla chips (the scoop kind are the best!).

Enjoy.

GLOSSARY

Aloha—Hawaiian for hello, love, and I'm outta here

A New York minute—catch it if you can

Black Friday—Angela's favorite shopping day of the year; sharpened elbows recommended

Blush—what people used to do when they were embarrassed

BTW—by the way

Conscious-pricker—things that make you go Hmmm…

Cooties—What cooties are to Donna, chiggers are to Shae

Ewww or Ewwe—what to say when you see roadkill, a really ugly pair of shoes, or female sheep

Foo-foo values—things under car hoods that make cars go

Fox urine—liquid scarecrow for mischievous rabbits

Grin—Something a person does just before she has to bare it, something Kitty does after digging his claws into a thigh.

Hawaii – paradise in the middle of the Pacific Ocean

Hello?—This place has no shoe stores?, It's as plain as your nose, Get real!, Does a bear poop in the woods?, Like…duh!

HRT—Hormone Replacement Therapy; causes uninterrupted, dry-sheet sleep for 8 hours

Kitty—orange domestic longhair cat; believes humans to be furniture

La Pergola—A+ but traditional classy Italian restaurant run by a family of dashing brothers clad in tuxedos who greet female guests with "Ciao Bella!" and a kiss on the hand. Out of business.

lol—laugh out loud

Maggie—short for Margaret Thatcher; happiest Old English Sheepdog on the planet

OCD—Obsessive Compulsive Disorder; a disease some writers suffer from, and TV detectives named Monk

Ooh—"Goody, goody," or "Oh, yuck!" (see ewww)

Ouch Chihuahua—Excited utterance by a Canadian shoe-aholic

Oy—"ohmygosh" with attitude

Pepto—pink stuff that makes your tummy feel better

Permission to be Human Day—International holiday of no set date; exists freely, can be invoked whenever needed

PMS—Periodic Mental Slump; attacks many females without warning

Prada—Way expensive clothing and shoe brand, and also what the devil wears (see book by Lauren Weisberger)

P.S.—Public School

Ruth's Chris—Such delicious steaks it turns vegans into meat-eaters

Scherenschnitte—German for papercutting designs; fun craft for those who don't like needles as in knitting or crochet

Whine—What most women have learned by age 10 and perfected by age 15 (same as "blank stare" for men)

Yada yada—And so forth and so on; blah, blah, blah; catch my drift, dot-dot-dot, quick way to edit word count...

Voilà!—French word for: Walla! Ta da!

@@—Rolling eyes heavenward;the eye roll, something Canadian blondes, southern belles, and all teenagers do quite frequently

^_^ —Tammy's happy face; just picture a halo over it

:-)—no worries

About the Writers

SHAE COOKE is grateful that even divorce could not separate her from the love of Jesus Christ. She writes from beautiful Anmore, British Columbia where her family and the magnificent natural wonders of her creative Father encourage her inspirational voice, heard in print worldwide. Additionally, Shae jumps into the shoes of others as a ghostwriter. A former foster child, a mother, and now in a beautiful relationship, the Lord holds copyright to her testimony, which is a work in progress. Write her at P.O. Box 78006, Port Coquitlam, B.C. Canada V3B 7H5 or visit www.shaecooke.com.

TAMMY FITZGERALD graduated from Cedarville University with a degree in English Literature, and went on to become an editor at Destiny Image Publishing Company. She also recently completed her teacher's certification at Shippensburg University. She currently lives in Pennsylvania with her cat, and has her eyes open to see where in the world God will lead her next. Contact her at tcfitzgerald1984@hotmail.com.

DONNA SCUDERI is a former high school English teacher and one-time rock musician who has been writing and editing professionally for more than a decade. Having served nine years in the editing department of an international ministry, she now serves a variety of individuals and organizations to perfect their message through print and public speaking. She also recently completed a feature-length screenplay. Contact Donna at readywriter77@yahoo.com.

ANGELA RICKABAUGH SHEARS has been writing and editing for more than 20 years, although this trip to The Powder Room is her first out-from-behind-the-scenes book. She earned her B.A. from the University of Hawaii Manoa with a major in journalism/communications and a minor in political science. Visit her Website at www.writewordsnow.com. She, her husband Darrell, and their Old English Sheepdog, Maggie, live in Southcentral Pennsylvania...except when they are daydreaming about living back in Hawaii.

RECOMMENDED READING

Called Together by Steve and Mary Prokopchak

Choosing to Wait by Laura Gallier

God Is Your Matchmaker by Stephanie Herzog

Lady in Waiting by Jackie Kendall and Debby Jones

Learning How to Trust Again by Ed Delph, Alan & Pauly Heller

Not Until He Left by Dionne Arceneaux

Opposites Attract by Carl Hampsch

Purity by Kris Vallotton

Sex Traps by Wanda Davis-Turner

Single, Married, Separated, and Life After Divorce by Myles Munroe

The Purpose of Power of Love and Marriage by Myles Munroe

Waiting and Dating by Myles Munroe

Wedlock or Deadlock? by Manickam Chandrakumar

What Guys See That Girls Don't by Sharon Daugherty